剑桥双语分级阅读·小说馆(第2版)

原版系列编辑 Philip Prowse

U0956674

Man Hunt

罪案追凶

[英] 理查德·麦克安德鲁 著

秦怡 编译

北京语言大学出版社
BEIJING LANGUAGE AND CULTURE UNIVERSITY PRESS

CAMBRIDGE UNIVERSITY PRESS

社图号25006

图书在版编目（CIP）数据

罪案追凶 ： 英汉对照 / （英） 理查德・麦克安德鲁 (Richard MacAndrew） 著 ； 秦怡编译. -- 2版. -- 北京 ： 北京语言大学出版社, 2025. 3. -- (剑桥双语分级阅读小说馆). -- ISBN 978-7-5619-6725-6

Ⅰ. H319.4

中国国家版本馆CIP数据核字第2025FG2994号

罪案追凶
ZUI'AN ZHUI XIONG

责任编辑：梁　骁
责任印制：周　燚

出版发行：北京语言大学出版社
社　　址：北京市海淀区学院路 15 号，100083
网　　址：www.blcup.com
电子信箱：service@blcup.com
电　　话：编 辑 部 010-8230 1019
发 行 部 010-8230 3650/3591/3648
北语书店 010-8230 3653
网购咨询 010-8230 3908
印　　刷：东港股份有限公司

版　　次：2017 年 6 月第 1 版　2025 年 3 月第 2 版　**印　　次**：2025 年 3 月第 1 次印刷
开　　本：880 毫米 × 1230 毫米　1/32　**印　　张**：6.375
字　　数：152 千字　**定　　价**：23.00 元

PRINTED IN CHINA

凡有印装质量问题，本社负责调换。售后QQ号1367565611，电话010-82303590

Preface

前言

“剑桥双语分级阅读·小说馆”是一套从剑桥大学出版社引进的面向非英语国家英语学习者的分级系列读物，由英语语言教学专家及小说作家合力创作。创作过程历时三十余年，出版后受到世界各地英语教师和英语学习者的喜爱，许多读本再版多次，三十余年来畅销不衰，成为受全球英语学习者青睐的优秀读本。

本系列读物具有以下突出特色：

1. 是原创英语读物，而非改编自普通作品的读物。因此，阅读本系列读物，我们读到的是原汁原味的原创英语，而非人为改编过的二手英语。

2. 是当代优秀短篇小说，而非年代久远的小说。因此，阅读本系列读物，我们读到的是当今鲜活的、学了就能用的英语，而非穿越时空的、学了用不上的英语；了解的是与读者同时代不同国家人们的生活和思想，而非隔代人的生活、文化和风土人情。

3. 是专为非英语国家的英语学习者量身定制的读物，而非为英语母语者所写的大众读物。因此，本系列读物是中国读者首选的英语学习读物。

4. 是英美知名小说家和英语语言教学专家合力创作的读物。小说家保障了读物的可读性与可欣赏性，英语语言教学专家保障了读物语言作为英语习得材料的科学性与可学性。本系列读物中的多个读本都曾在世界上颇具影响力的“语言学习者文学奖”（Language Learner Literature Award）评选中获得大奖。因此，阅读本系列读物，我们会在欣赏小说的同时，自然而然地、有效地提高自己的英语水平。

5. 本系列读物的故事题材丰富多样，包括侦探、情感、历险、悬疑、人文、科幻、喜剧等，读者可以随心选择自己喜欢的类别阅读；故事内容生动有趣，故事情节引人入胜、扣人心弦，读者一旦开始阅读，就想一口气读完，使阅读真正升华到“悦读”。

6. 随书附赠的音频材料内容精彩，是专业配音员的演绎再创作。听着它，我们犹如在听广播剧、听评书，又仿佛是在听电影、听话剧……这种聆听英语的享受将彻底扫除学生对英语听力的畏难心理。

7. 本系列读物所使用的语言，既有英式英语，也有美式英语，对应的音频材料也相应分为英音和美音，读者可根据自己的喜好来选择。

8. 本系列近百本读物根据《欧洲语言共同参考框架》(CEFR) 和剑桥大学外语考评部开发的 ESOL 考试的标准来确定级别划分，是建立在科学研究和实践基础之上的分级。全套共分七个级别（与中国学生英语基础水平的大致对应关系，请参见图书封底表格），读者可根据自己的英语基础选择相应级别的读本来学习。

为了更好地帮助中国学生学习和欣赏，“剑桥双语分级阅读 · 小说馆”从剑桥大学出版社原版引进后又增加了以下内容：

1. 增加了适量的辅助学习内容，包括“读前思考”“读后活动”“学习指导”三个板块，其中“学习指导”板块又包括生词、短语和表达、文化点滴、阅读练习四项内容。增加这些板块的目的是全方位帮助学生提升英语阅读能力，扩充词汇量，扫除阅读中的文化障碍，增强对英语小说的鉴赏能力。

2. 增加了小说全文的参考译文。出于语言学习的考虑，译文多采用直译，但也尽量符合中文的表达习惯。

值得一提的是，所增加的辅助学习内容和参考译文，全部由来自全国不同省市知名中学（包括人大附中、北大附中、清华附中、黄冈中学、上海中学等三十余所中学）的一线英语教师完成。这些一线教师的加盟，确保了所加内容与中国学生的英语学习特点和学习需求相吻合，为学生阅读和欣赏读物、提高英语水平给予恰到好处的助力。

英语阅读是英语课堂的延伸和补充，也是培养英语语感、提高英语水平的有效途径。选择一套好的英语读物，收获的将不仅仅是语言的进步。欢迎年轻朋友们来到“剑桥双语分级阅读·小说馆”，打开一本本好书，品味一个个好故事，为实现梦想搭建桥梁。

北京语言大学出版社

Contents 目录

People in the story

故事中的人物

Detective Inspector (DI) Charles Neville: a police officer

刑侦督察查尔斯·内维尔：一名警官

Detective Sergeant (DS) Helen Scott: a police officer

刑侦警长海伦·斯科特：一名警官

Fiona Russell: a crime analyst

菲奥娜·拉塞尔：一名犯罪分析师

Kay Harding: a police doctor

凯·哈丁：一名法医

Jonathan Greene: a journalist
乔纳森·格林：一名新闻记者

Alan Reid: an army major
艾伦·里德：一名陆军少校

Terry Reid: Alan's brother
特里·里德：艾伦的弟弟

Mrs Reid: Terry and Alan's mother
里德夫人：特里和艾伦的母亲

Before reading

读前思考

1. What is a 'man hunt'?
2. Describe the image you see on the front cover. What do you think it means?
3. Read the back cover blurb. What kind of story is it?
4. Look at the list of characters on pages 2 and 3. How could you divide them into three groups?
5. If you have the recording, listen to Chapter 1.

Chapter 1
A moorland death

The first killing went well. Perfectly, in fact. Though I always knew it would. I had planned it well. Arrangements, organisation – these are things I'm good at. Now I've discovered I'm good at killing too.

At six o'clock in the morning I turned the car left off the road towards Tan Hill. The highest pub in England is at Tan Hill. But there's just the pub there, nothing else – no houses, no other buildings. The nearest village is eight kilometres away, the nearest shop twelve kilometres. This is wild, treeless country. There would be amazing views later, when the sun got up, but I wasn't interested in them.

I continued along a dirt road across moorland, stopping only when the car could no longer be seen from the road. Not that there was ever much traffic here.

I got out and stretched, enjoying the sharp cold of the early autumn air. To make myself less noticeable against the dull green grasses of the countryside around me, I was wearing hiking clothes and boots of a similar greeny colour. I took an old brown backpack off the back seat of the car and checked inside. There was a map, a bottle of water, gloves, binoculars and some sandwiches. I took out the gloves and put them on. I also had a hand-held GPS – there were no paths where I was going. In more ways than one I was making my way into the unknown. It was a journey of discovery, one that I had promised myself for some time.

It took me two hours to walk across the wild moorland to where I wanted to be – two hours that seemed like no time at all. Excitement and nervousness were building up inside me in equal measure. In my mind I was going through the different possibilities of what might happen – yet I knew I would be successful.

Finally I arrived at the place I had chosen. There was an old, long-empty house beside a dirty-brown stream, which laughed its way down the side of the hill. The house was roofless and one wall was falling down. There were piles of old stones lying around. I found a stone that felt comfortable in my right hand, heavy and with sharp edges. Later I would use it.

A path turned this way and that up the hillside, past the house and over a wooden bridge across the stream. The path is well known to walkers, though not especially popular. The chances of a single walker taking advantage of this bright autumn morning were good, but there was unlikely to be a whole crowd of them. Then later, when the body was found, the police would think the killer had come along the same path as the walker, rather than over the pathless moorland. They would start searching in the wrong places. I had chosen well.

I took off my gloves, got my binoculars and a sandwich out of my backpack, and sat down on a large stone to wait. From where I was, I would be able to see anyone coming from a long way away, but they would have difficulty seeing me.

I had hardly finished my sandwich when a man appeared in the distance, walking in my direction. Quickly I put on my gloves, picked up my chosen stone and hid behind the back wall of the house. I waited. My heart went faster. I took deep breaths to slow it down. I had a picture in my mind of the man coming nearer. My excitement rose; my nervousness disappeared. I heard the sound of footsteps on the dirt path. Coming near. Nearer. I raised my stone. This was the moment of truth.

And then it was done.

The man lay on his side on the ground by my feet. His longish grey hair had fallen over his face. His eyes were closed, but there was movement under the eyelids. I took off my left glove and felt the side of his neck. He wasn't dead, just unconscious. I looked at him. This was the moment – the moment I wanted to experience, the moment I had promised myself. I hit him again, hard, driving the edge of the stone deep into the side of his head through the bone. And then he was completely still.

I looked down at the man. A thousand different feelings fought for my attention. I had done it! I felt high, drunk, untouchable. I felt brilliant, strong, undefeatable. I was alive.

I threw the stone far away. Let the police find it, I thought. They would learn nothing from it.

Then I took a playing card out of my jacket pocket, found the dead man's wallet in his jacket and put the card inside. I put the wallet back where I had found it.

A moment later I picked up my backpack and started back to my car.

This is just the beginning. I can show them. I can show them they are wrong. I can show them what I'm really made of.

* * *

It was four o'clock in the afternoon when Detective Inspector Charles Neville got out of a dark blue police Land Rover in the middle of the cold North Yorkshire moorland near Surrender Bridge. The emergency call reporting a dead body had come in an hour or so earlier. The first police officers had arrived at the scene twenty minutes later and established that the death wasn't natural. Neville had immediately been called out. It was his day off and he had been out with his wife. Shopping for a new kitchen for his home suddenly seemed far less important.

As Neville got out of the vehicle, a young woman with short dark hair came over to him. It was his sergeant, Helen Scott.

'I got here a few minutes ago,' said Scott. 'The body's over there behind that building.' She waved a hand in the direction of an old roofless building that had half fallen down.

Neville could see that black and yellow scene-of-crime tape had already been put around the building, and also round a largish area of moorland. Three other Land Rovers and a couple of other off-road vehicles were parked near the building.

As Neville walked with Scott towards the building, he looked up at the sky. Thick dark cloud was beginning to blow in from the west.

'Yorkshire weather,' he said bad-temperedly, pointing at the sky. 'Let's hope the rain keeps away until we're finished here.'

Neville was from the South-East. Although he'd lived in Yorkshire for the last ten years, he still hadn't got used to the weather. When the sun was out, it was indeed a special place, but it wasn't uncommon to experience all four seasons in one day.

'Yes,' agreed Scott.

Around the corner of the building they found Kay Harding, the police doctor, bending over the body of a middle-aged man dressed in hiking clothes and boots. He still had a backpack on. Harding stood up as she heard the detectives arrive and started talking immediately.

'Charles, Helen,' she said, looking from one to the other and then down at the body. 'What we have here is the body of a fifty- to fifty-five-year-old man. He was presumably out walking. Someone has hit him hard on the side of the head twice. Probably with a stone.'

'Time of death?' asked Neville.

'Somewhere between eight and ten this morning, I'd say,' replied Harding.

'Anything else?' asked Neville.

'Not at the moment,' replied Harding. 'Once the photographer's done his business, I'll take the body away. I'll leave you the backpack and anything I find in his pockets.'

'OK. Thanks,' said Neville. Neville's mood improved. Harding was one of the best – clear, professional, and she didn't waste words. He liked that. He looked at the sky again and then at his watch. They would have to hurry. He turned to Scott.

'We'll have enough daylight,' he said, 'but God knows how long the rain will hold off. Get this area searched – as much as you can and as carefully as you can. We're obviously looking for anything that might be useful, but we're especially looking for the stone that killed him.'

'Right,' answered Scott.

'Who found the body?' asked Neville.

'A local couple,' answered Scott. 'They're in the green Land Rover over there.' She pointed to it.

'I'll go and talk to them,' said Neville. 'Then we'll need to think about an operations room. Reeth is the nearest village. Maybe there's somewhere there.'

Scott nodded. She and Neville had offices at the police station in Richmond, the nearest town, but that was almost twenty kilometres away. Neville would want to be closer to the scene than that. There was a mobile office they could bring over and use, or they could find a large room nearby that they could borrow.

'Right,' she said. 'I'll get the search started here.'

* * *

At eight o'clock the following morning Neville and Scott and a team of fifteen officers met in Reeth Memorial Hall, their new operations room. This large empty room was normally used for anything from children's playgroups, to concerts, to band practice. Now it was filled with desks, chairs, computers, phones and police officers.

Neville stood facing his team, his age showing in the grey of his hair and the lines on his face. Scott was next to him. Neither of them had had much sleep. Behind them was a whiteboard with the photograph of a man's face on it.

'OK,' began Neville. 'First, what we know. This is Matthew Kenworthy.'

He pointed at the photograph.

'He was found at three o'clock yesterday afternoon by a local couple who were out walking their dog. He died some time yesterday morning between eight and ten. Someone hit him on the side of the head twice with a stone. We've got the stone, but it's anyone's guess if we'll find out anything from it.'

He stepped back and looked across at Scott.

'Over to you,' he said.

'Kenworthy was here on his own, on a walking holiday,' she began. 'He was staying at the Shoulder of Mutton pub here in Reeth. He arrived a couple of days ago. He hadn't been to the area before. He was friendly, but kept himself to himself.'

She cleared her throat before continuing.

'Yesterday morning he went off in his car, intending to walk an eight-kilometre path that goes in a circle from Surrender Bridge. We found his car near the bridge.'

Scott then pointed to a number of plastic bags on the table beside her.

'We've been through the things in his room. There's nothing of interest there. We've been through what he had with him on the walk. He just had the usual stuff that walkers take – map, GPS, hat, gloves, sandwiches, water – but there was one unusual thing.'

Scott picked up a plastic bag and held it up so that everyone could see. Inside the bag was a playing card.

'The ace of spades,' she said. 'It was in his wallet. And there were no other cards in his room. Any ideas?'

Heads shook all round the room.

Neville stepped forward again.

'OK,' he said. 'Kenworthy was single and lived in Bristol. The police there are making inquiries. Up here we've got work to do too. I want four of you to walk the eight kilometres that Kenworthy intended to walk. The murderer may have followed him or may have come from the opposite direction. Go in two pairs – one pair in the same direction as Kenworthy, the other pair in the opposite direction. Check along the path for anything that might be useful.'

Neville picked up a pile of photographs from the table and gave them to Scott.

'I want the rest of you making door-to-door inquiries in Reeth,' he said. 'It's a small place. Everyone knows everyone. Take Kenworthy's picture with you. See if anyone knows him, or spoke to him, or saw anyone speaking to him. DS Scott will tell you who's doing what.'

Neville turned and was about to leave the room when a voice came from the back.

'Sir.'

Neville turned round.

'Yes?' he said.

One of the officers had a hand in the air to show

that he had spoken.

'What is it?' asked Neville.

'The ace of spades, sir,' said the officer. 'I've just remembered – it's the card of death.'

Chapter 2
A serial killer?

I waited ten days before I decided to kill again. I could have waited longer, but I wanted to experience that wonderful feeling again. I wanted to experience it quite badly. That feeling of pleasure, of being successful, and of showing I'm right. I've read the papers and the police seem to have no idea what's happening. I didn't think there was any danger of being found out. I was right about that.

I decided to use the same basic plan as before. I would park my car in one place and then find an 'unwilling helper' somewhere completely different.

However, I had made some improvements to my plan. The first was to leave my car in full view somewhere. Hikers leave their cars all over the North Yorkshire countryside. No one pays them any attention. But a car that appears to be hidden might now, after what happened ten days ago, be of great interest to the police.

Secondly, I was going to put my plan into action in the late afternoon. I hoped that meant the body wouldn't be found until the next morning. That would make things a little more difficult for the police.

Another change was to use a knife. I had decided I wanted to experience different ways of killing.

Finally, I was going to use footpaths to get to the place I had chosen. There are so many paths all over this part of Yorkshire, it would be difficult to avoid them for ever. Of course, the police might be able to match my boots or my clothes to something they found along the path. But I had thought about that. After this and every future adventure I would burn everything that I was wearing or carrying. Clever, aren't I? Cleverer than the police, I think.

I drove up the road from Grinton towards Redmire and left my car on moorland about halfway between the two villages. Then I started walking back over the hill towards Reeth. The day was cloudy, but it was warm for the time of year.

The countryside in the Yorkshire Dales is very beautiful: hills and dales, up and down, wild moorland on the tops of the hills, sleepy villages and farms in the dales at the bottom. To Yorkshire people Yorkshire is 'God's own country'. But I wasn't there to enjoy the natural beauty.

It took me a couple of hours walking through completely empty moorland to reach the place I was looking for – a small building. Normally empty, it was sometimes used by groups of people out shooting birds – but not today. It was right beside one of the main paths in the area with wonderful long views each way up and down the valley.

I took my knife and a map out of my backpack and sat down behind the building to wait. There was always a chance that this late in the day nobody would walk past me. However, that was a chance I was prepared to take.

After about half an hour, I saw a man and a woman in the distance, but they turned off before they reached me and walked down the hill to the river at the bottom. That was lucky because it might have been difficult to kill both of them. I was saving a double killing for the time when I would use a gun.

Shortly after that, I noticed a woman on her own coming from the opposite direction. It soon became clear she was going to come right past me. This time I felt very calm. I knew what to do. Time seemed to move more slowly. As the woman walked towards the building, I prepared myself and began to look forward to what I was going to do.

She was still about fifty metres away when I stepped out. I was holding the map in my hand. The knife was in the same hand, but hidden under the map. As I stepped out, I was looking at the map so as not to frighten her. She kept on walking towards me and I looked up. She was medium height, blonde, probably in her thirties.

I smiled at her and looked a bit embarrassed.

'I'm sorry,' I said, waving the map a little, but keeping the knife hidden. 'I seem to be a bit lost. You couldn't show me where I am, could you?'

'Of course,' she said and came over to where I was standing.

She bent to look at the map and I stuck my knife sharply into the left-hand side of her chest.

There was a long, soft noise as the air seemed to leave her body. I looked into her eyes, feeling the moment, enjoying it. A surprised look crossed her face. She tried to speak, but couldn't. I let go of the knife as she fell to her knees, then onto her side. Her eyes closed and she was dead. I stood still for a moment looking down at her. I had done it again! I felt wonderful. God-like.

Quickly I bent down and pulled the knife out of her chest. I cleaned it on the outside of her jacket, then put it in my backpack. I took out a playing card from my pocket and put it in one of her pockets. Just so that the police would know who had done it.

Then I started the two-hour walk back to my car. Two happy hours in which I could relive the moment.

* * *

Fiona Russell was in her office in the North Yorkshire Police Headquarters in Northallerton. She had just finished reading a recent report about internet crime and sat back to think about what she had learnt. Although she worked for the police, she wasn't actually a police officer. She was a crime analyst. That meant she was one of the few people who was likely to see everything to do with a particular crime. She read every piece of paper, every interview, every report. She looked for patterns, similarities, differences. She reported her findings to the senior officer in the investigation, and she would make suggestions about what else needed to be done or what further information might be useful.

Just as she sat back, her phone rang.

'Russell,' she said, picking up the phone

immediately.

'This is Detective Inspector Neville, North Yorkshire Police,' said the voice, coming straight to the point. 'I'm looking for an analyst with experience of serial killers. Your boss tells me you're the person to speak to.'

Russell felt the hairs on the back of her neck stand up. She had worked on two serial killer investigations before. At the end of each she had been exhausted. Each investigation had been a race against time; a race to stop the killer murdering yet more people. Each investigation had demanded long, patient hours; each had stretched her mind more than she thought possible. Each had, in its own way, given her a new and different way of looking at pain and suffering; but each had brought its own excitement and professional pleasure.

'I guess so,' replied Russell.

'Good,' said Neville. 'At the moment we've only got two murders so, if we're going by the rules, this person isn't yet a serial killer.'

Russell knew that for a killer to become 'serial' the rule was three or more.

'But I don't want to wait for number three,' continued Neville. 'There's no doubt in my mind there will be a third one and more if we don't find him. You'll understand why when you see what we've got so far. I'd like you on the team as soon as possible.'

Russell noticed Neville's use of 'him'. There had been female serial killers – but mostly they were men.

'OK,' answered Russell. 'Where are you?'

'Reeth, Swaledale,' replied Neville.

Russell looked at her watch. 'I can be there in about an hour,' she said.

* * *

Ninety minutes later Fiona Russell was sitting at a table at the back of the operations room. Helen Scott was in a chair opposite, giving her a quick overview of the investigation so far. She was already describing the second murder.

'The body was found early this morning on the hillside just outside Reeth,' she said. 'I'll show you where on the map in a moment. It was a thirty-two-year-old woman, Sheila McFadyen. She lived in Richmond. She was a nurse. She worked nights at the local hospital and often came over here during the day to go walking. She was divorced. Her ex-husband lives locally, but they seem to have got on well enough. He says he was at home at the time she was murdered. On his own. It seems unlikely he's our man, but we're checking him out anyway – just to be on the safe side. She didn't have a boyfriend – at least not that anyone knows about. She had a lot of friends. Everyone speaks well of her.'

She held her hands out as if to show the hopelessness of the situation.

'There appears to be no reason why anyone would want to kill her,' Scott added.

She paused for a moment.

'What about the crime scene?' asked Russell.

'Like the first one, we've got almost nothing,' continued Scott. 'The killer stuck a knife straight into McFadyen's heart. We haven't found the knife. The killer pulled it out, cleaned it on her jacket and took it away. We've found nothing at the scene that tells us anything about the killer. We don't know which way he arrived at the scene or which way he left. Actually, we don't know if it's a man or a woman. Nobody seems to have seen anything or anyone strange.'

Scott reached over to a neighbouring table and picked up two small plastic bags. Inside each was a playing card – an ace of spades in one, the two of spades in the other.

'And then we have these,' she said and put them on the table in front of Russell. Russell picked one up and looked at it.

Scott sat back in her chair and looked at Russell.

'Two playing cards,' said Scott. 'The ace was found on the first body, the two on the second. You can see why the boss thinks we've got a serial killer on our hands. Of course, the cards are a common make. Available anywhere.'

'Yes,' said Russell, as she put down the ace and picked up the two. Looking at the two of spades, she noticed two handwritten words in the middle of the card. They read 'By knife'. An icy feeling ran down her back.

She put down the card and looked at Scott. She was in her late twenties, with short dark hair, smartly dressed and clearly intelligent. A useful person to have in this kind of investigation. Everyone needed to be awake and alive to all the possibilities. She was about to speak when a tall man in a suit came towards them. His face was lined and there was a lot of grey in his black hair.

'DI Neville,' he said, introducing himself. 'Call me Charles. You must be Fiona Russell.'

He pulled a chair out from the table and sat down.

'Has Helen told you where we're at?' he asked.

'Yes, she has,' answered Russell.

'And?' asked Neville. 'Any immediate thoughts?'

Russell was unwilling to say too much until she knew more about the investigation. However, being new to the team, she felt she needed to give Neville and Scott something. Having read widely about serial killers, she could make a few general points.

'We can make some intelligent guesses,' said Russell. 'First of all, we're most probably looking for a man. Most serial killers are men. There have been women serial killers but, interestingly, they usually prefer to kill indoors – inside the home or maybe in a hospital – a nurse killing off patients, for example.'

Russell looked at Scott and Neville.

'And I'd guess he's between the ages of twenty-five and forty,' she continued. 'He needs to be old enough to plan and organise this. But when they're over forty, people normally calm down, or they've already been caught and locked up.'

Neville and Scott looked at each other, then back at Russell.

'And he does seem to be organised,' added Russell. 'Organised and intelligent. That's why you've found so little at the crime scenes. He's also carried out the murders well away from any CCTV cameras. We're the most watched country in the world, but out here in the Dales there are very few cameras at all – not many CCTV traffic cameras in towns, hardly any cameras around buildings. And out in the countryside none at all.'

Neville and Scott were listening and watching carefully.

'I'd also say we're looking for someone reasonably local – someone who knows the area,' Russell went on. 'I mean, I'm sure you've thought of this yourselves. Both the murders happened in places where the killer was unlikely to be interrupted. He obviously knows the area well.'

'True,' said Scott, putting her elbows on the table. 'But why? Why have these people been killed?'

'I'm not a psychologist,' said Russell. 'I just study the facts. But, looking at the playing cards, I agree with you that he'll try again. I think you're absolutely right that this is a serial killer.'

She looked at both of them and gave a small smile.

'And, of course, if he keeps killing, we'll catch him. We only need to get lucky once. He has to stay lucky all the time.'

* * *

That afternoon the restaurant at the nearby Half Moon Hotel was full of journalists, both national and local, from the newspapers, radio and TV. Charles Neville, standing and facing the room, had explained the latest developments – the finding of the second body and how the investigation was moving forward. He didn't much like talking to journalists – in fact he didn't much like journalists – but he knew that there were times when they could help investigations. He had given a short report to keep them happy, but said nothing about the playing cards. It was usual for the police to keep back some information. This unreported information was often useful later.

Now he was preparing to answer questions. With two dead bodies and no idea who the killer might be, he wasn't expecting an easy time. He could see Scott at the back of the room standing and watching. She smiled at him to let him know she was there if he needed her. He nodded his thanks.

'I've just time for a few questions,' said Neville, looking around the room. A few people asked for more information about where the bodies had been found; someone else asked some questions about the dead man and woman. Then a woman at the front spoke.

'Gemma Taylor. Radio Yorkshire,' she said. 'There have been two murders so far. Do you think this is the work of a serial killer?'

Neville took a breath before answering.

'As you know, the two people were killed in very different ways,' he said. 'However, we're obviously keeping an open mind on this question.'

A man near the back raised a hand.

'Jonathan Greene. *London Evening Post*. Isn't it true that a playing card was found at each crime scene? Wouldn't that suggest the same killer for both crimes?'

The room had been reasonably quiet, but now there was complete silence. This was new information. Neville's neck started to turn red. Scott could see that he was holding back his anger. Neville caught Scott's attention at the back of the room. She knew what he wanted and nodded at him.

'I'm afraid I can't discuss exactly what was and wasn't found at the crime scenes,' said Neville.

But Greene wasn't giving up so easily.

'Surely playing cards found at each crime scene would suggest the same killer?' said Greene. 'Possibly even a serial killer.'

Suddenly all the journalists started talking to each other. Two left the room, walking past Scott, taking phones from their pockets as they went.

'This second investigation is less than a day old. We don't yet have a clear idea of how everything at the crime scene might be important,' said Neville. He looked at his watch. 'And now, ladies and gentlemen, I'm afraid that's all I have time for.'

He looked at Scott and nodded, then left the room quickly. There was a lot of noise as the journalists stood up and started to leave. When Jonathan Greene stood up, Scott noticed he was short, rather fat, with thinning light brown hair and a big nose. Not attractive. As he walked past her, she turned and walked along beside him.

'Mr Greene,' she said. 'I'm Detective Sergeant Scott. I'd like to have a word with you.'

Chapter 3 Early investigations

What a good idea it was to send a text message to that journalist! Of course, he won't know who it's from. I used a special website – aliamail.com. You can use it to send emails and text messages without anyone knowing where they come from. You have to give a name and an email address when you start using the website, but I gave a false name and I used an internet email service. I also sent the message from an internet café, not from my own computer. Smart, eh?

Naturally, the police will want to talk to everyone who knows the journalist's mobile phone number. That could be hundreds of people. And anyway, the police won't find my name. The journalist has no idea that I know his number. How, in fact, do I know it? Well, that's my secret.

So, soon I will have what I want. The information about the playing cards will be in tomorrow's papers. Then the whole country will know that these achievements are the work of one person. The whole country will see how good I am at what I do, how successful I can be. And then eventually, when I reach my final goal, I will show them that they were wrong. Who are 'they'? They are the people who stopped me realising the one burning ambition I had in life. They are the people who wrongly and unkindly took away the chance I had to achieve something real.

But I'm talking too much and, as the saying goes, 'Actions speak louder than words.' I must get on and plan my next adventure.

First I need some new clothes and boots. I burned the clothes I used last time – as I said I would – and the boots are at the bottom of the River Swale with a heavy stone in each one. I don't want to buy new clothes. Second-hand ones will be much better. There are plenty of shops around selling second-hand clothes. For a start second-hand clothes are cheaper – and after all I'm only going to wear them once; but also no one will recognise them as being mine. That should confuse the police if they ever get a description of me.

Then I've got to decide the 'how', 'when' and 'where' for my next adventure. The 'how' is easy. This time I want to get up close and personal. A strangling, my hands around the throat of my 'helper'. I want to experience the physical closeness that comes from using my hands rather than a stone or a knife. So far I have always watched life go. This time I want to feel it leave.

As for the 'when', it must be soon, I think. I can't wait much longer. The police are no closer to finding me. I don't have to worry about them. And I have a growing hunger for the excitement of the kill. Or is it a thirst – for blood? To be honest, I don't care. For me it has become like a drug – one which I need more and more.

So there's only one thing left to decide: the 'where'. I'll have to study my map. The Yorkshire Dales is a large area, but fortunately I know it well. It will be easy to find somewhere suitable. You might want to know where, but I'm not going to tell you. You'll find out soon enough. A quiet place for a private meeting.

* * *

'I tell you – I don't know who sent it to me.' Jonathan Greene searched through his pockets and finally pulled out a mobile phone. Greene, Neville and Scott were at the back of the Reeth Memorial Hall in a small room which Neville had decided to use for interviews. There were four chairs and a table; the walls were a dull cream colour with some tourist photos of Swaledale on them, and there was a window that looked out onto the back of Reeth Garage.

Greene put his phone on the table and pushed it across to Neville.

'Check for yourself,' he said rather crossly. 'There's no sender's number.'

Neville pushed the phone towards Scott. She picked it up, opened it and started pressing buttons.

'You didn't think it might be a good idea to come and talk to me, the senior officer, about it?' Neville's face was still red with anger, and there was a sharp edge to his voice.

'Come on, Inspector,' replied Greene. He put an elbow on the table and turned his hand over. 'I'm a journalist. I get a text message with information about a murder inquiry – information that the police must already have. Do I go and tell the police something they already know, or do I send in the story so that the *Evening Post* is first with the breaking news? Come on, Inspector! Get real!'

'Don't tell me to get real!' exploded Neville. His fist hit the table hard, his face grew darker. 'This is a murder investigation.' Neville spoke slowly, his voice low and angry, his eyes locked on to Greene's. 'You have what could be, in fact probably is, a message directly from the murderer. You have no idea how important that might be to the investigation. It might lead us straight to the murderer. It might help us save a life, lives even. And yet you don't think that the first thing you should do is bring it to the attention of the police? No, Mr Greene. You get real. Keeping information from the police is a crime – and you know it.'

Neville stopped speaking, but continued to stare at Greene. There was silence in the room. Eventually Greene looked away, embarrassed, even a little shaken by Neville's anger.

Scott looked up for a moment and then continued to examine the phone.

'He's right,' she said to Neville. 'There's no sender number on that message.'

'How easy is it to get your number?' asked Neville. 'How many people have it?'

'Not that many,' replied Greene, looking happier now that the questioning had moved onto easier ground. 'Probably just the people in my phone book. I don't give my number out to that many people. And the newspaper won't give it out.'

Neville looked at Scott.

'We'll want that phone then,' he said. 'Make sure you give Mr Greene a receipt for it and get someone to check everyone in his phone book.'

'But, hey, you can't do that,' said Greene. 'I need my phone.'

'Tough,' said Neville, turning back to Greene. 'It's part of a murder inquiry. Now get out. You're lucky not to be spending the night in jail. And next time – if there is a next time – make sure you do the right thing.'

Greene stood up slowly and, shaking his head, left the room. As the door closed, Neville looked at Scott.

'Check him out too,' said Neville. 'And actually, do it yourself. I want someone experienced on it. I want to know how long he's been a journalist, if he's any good, how long he's been at the *London Evening Post*. Everything. I want to know why the murderer chose to give the information to him. If, in fact, he did.'

Scott looked up sharply.

'You don't think he's ...?' she began.

'Probably not,' replied Neville. 'But it doesn't hurt to be careful.'

* * *

Late afternoon the following day, with the second

murder less than forty-eight hours old, Russell was called into the interview room to talk to Neville and Scott. A lot of noise was coming through from the main hall. Officers were making phone calls, asking questions, checking information, writing reports. Neville closed the door and the noise level dropped.

'Right,' he said, pulling out a chair and sitting down heavily. 'Fiona, you've been here twenty-four hours now. And you've been through everything. What can you tell us?'

Russell sat down. Scott took out a notebook and kept it in her hand. Russell had a pile of papers, which she put on the table.

'Well, I don't want to raise your hopes too much,' began Russell, 'but there is a line of inquiry that might be useful. Though "might" is the important word here.'

'Go on,' said Neville.

'The Bristol police have been very helpful,' continued Russell. 'They've searched Kenworthy's house, spoken to a lot of his friends and to his employers. Kenworthy worked at one of the universities in Bristol. He was a lecturer in medicine at Avon University.'

'And Sheila McFadyen was a nurse,' said Scott.

'Exactly,' replied Russell. 'But there's more. She actually did her nursing training at Avon University.'

'So she could have known Matthew Kenworthy?' said Neville.

'Well, yes.' Russell sounded unsure.

'But ...?' asked Neville.

'Like I said,' Russell went on, 'I don't want to raise your hopes. Sheila McFadyen was at university twelve, fifteen years ago. I don't yet know if Kenworthy was there then. He lectured in medicine; she studied nursing. OK, the subjects are similar, but they're completely different courses, so even if they were both there at the same time, they might not have known each other.'

'I see what you mean about "might" being the important word,' said Neville. 'However, it's certainly a line of inquiry that's worth following up.'

'Right,' replied Russell. 'I've emailed the Bristol police a list of questions that they can find answers to there. First thing tomorrow morning I'll have another list of questions that your officers can follow up here.'

'Good,' said Neville. 'Anything else?'

'Not really,' replied Russell. 'As I said yesterday, the killer is organised and intelligent. He's left us very little so far.'

'What about McFadyen's ex-husband?' asked Scott.

'Is there any chance it could be him? He kills someone else first, then his ex-wife, then a third person maybe – so it looks like a serial killing, but actually all he wants to do is get rid of his ex.'

'An unpleasant thought,' said Neville. The smallest of smiles came and went in his eyes. 'But one that's certainly worth considering. Why don't you look into that possibility?'

'OK,' replied Scott and wrote in her notebook.

Neville sat back in his chair.

'Now then,' he said, still looking at Scott. 'What about Mr Greene? Tell us what you've found out about him.'

Scott turned back a few pages in her notebook.

'Apparently Jonathan Greene is a well-known journalist. He works mainly down south on the *London Evening Post*, which explains why I've never heard of him.' Scott looked up from her notes. 'He usually covers crime stories, but he also makes his own investigations into areas where he thinks people have been breaking or bending the law.'

'Such as?' asked Neville.

'I've got a list of some of his more recent stories,' replied Scott, turning over a page in her notebook. 'A lot of his stuff is just straight crime reporting – what happened, who did what, who went to prison, that sort of thing. But at the end of last year he wrote a couple of big pieces. One was on crime in the health service – cleaners stealing drugs and equipment and selling it all on the black market. That resulted in a police investigation.'

'I remember that,' said Neville. 'I didn't realise it was Greene.'

'The other piece was an interview with Jerry Anderson,' continued Scott.

'Who's he?' asked Russell.

'One of the big players in organised crime in London in the 1980s,' answered Neville.

'He'd just come out of prison after fifteen years for bank robbery and murder,' continued Scott, 'and Greene persuaded him to do an interview. He talked all sorts of rubbish about how he had seen the light, given up his life of crime and was going to go straight.'

'Mind you,' added Neville, 'I'm told there's a few million that still hasn't been found from his last bank job, so he can probably afford to go straight.'

'Anyway, I guess that's why Greene's phone number is difficult to get hold of,' explained Scott. 'You wouldn't want Anderson calling you up in the middle of the night. He's not a pleasant character at the best of times.'

'Absolutely,' replied Neville.

Scott looked down at her notes again.

'And there's another big story that he's been working on recently,' she said. 'Unfortunately it hasn't made the newspapers yet, and as a result I haven't been able to find out anything about it. He was away for a couple of weeks at the beginning of the year working on something, but ... well, the people I spoke to either didn't know, or didn't want to tell me.'

'I think you should investigate that further,' suggested Russell. 'It might be worth finding out if that's why he's really up here. I mean, it seems odd for a journalist from a London evening newspaper to be here.'

'He might have come because of the text message,' said Scott.

'I don't think so,' replied Russell. She looked through some of the papers on the table in front of her. 'No,' she continued. 'He only received the message a couple of hours before Charles spoke to the journalists. I made a note of the time.'

'Well, I agree with Fiona,' said Neville. 'You need to find out more about this story of Greene's.'

Just then there was a knock. A woman with short blonde hair opened the door and looked into the room.

'Sorry to interrupt, sir,' she said to Neville. 'Another body's been found. An oldish man. On the Harkerside road, near Scabba Wath Bridge. There was a three of spades in his hand.'

Chapter 4
A different kind of killing

I needed luck today. I wasn't absolutely ready for the kill. I'd looked at my map. I had some ideas, but I hadn't reached a final decision on where I was going to find my 'helper'.

Then he found me!

I knew him, of course. He lived near me. I'd seen him around and chatted to him before. I passed him on the street near his house in the middle of the afternoon and said hello. He invited me in for a cup of tea and I accepted.

As soon as we stepped into his house, I knew he was the one. Something in the air seemed different. He was an ex-policeman and he knew something. I was sure of it. I experienced an unusual feeling, partly a warning, partly a call to action.

He turned and started to speak. Immediately I knew what I had to do. He looked in good shape for someone in his early sixties. But I'm young, strong and healthy, and I had the element of surprise on my side. To delay would allow the tiniest possibility of watching my dream die. I couldn't let that happen.

My hands flew forward round his neck. My thumbs pressed hard down on his throat, stopping him breathing. His eyes opened wide and filled with fear as he realised what I was doing.

He fought back. He tried to pull my hands away from his throat, but I was too strong. He hit at my arms, but he was already becoming weak. He reached for my eyes with his fingernails, a last hopeless attempt to save himself.

But I was expecting that. My head shot forward through his hands, my forehead hitting him square on the nose. There was the sickening noise of breaking bone. His hands fell weakly down to his sides, as his face started to turn a kind of bluish purple. A few drops of blood from his nose covered his top lip. His tongue came out. His body became a dead weight in my hands. I let it down gently and laid him on the floor.

Then I sat down next to him. I was breathing hard, my heart going as if I had just run a hundred metres. I could feel the sweat on my face and the fear in my heart. Fear? Or was it excitement?

I took some deep breaths and began to feel calmer. I looked at him. I felt his neck. He was definitely dead.

But I couldn't enjoy the moment as I'd hoped. I had a decision to make. I could leave the body here. Or I could take it into the countryside where the other bodies had been found.

I looked round. There was only a little blood. It was all on his top lip and drying fast. There were no obvious signs of a fight. Nothing to show that I had been there. But I'm a planner, a careful planner. I knew that the more I planned, the luckier I would be. So I decided to take the body to the countryside. Sure, the police would realise that the body had been moved – I had watched enough crime shows on TV to know that. But they wouldn't know where the body had been moved from. And that might be important. There might be just some little thing in this room – skin, hair, clothing – that could lead the police to me. But not if they didn't look!

It was a good plan. I felt a wave of pleasure wash over me.

I let myself out of the back door and started to walk home. I would need to steal a car – I obviously couldn't use my car for this. I'd also need a blanket to cover the body in the back of the car, and the three of spades.

* * *

Helen Scott pulled the police Land Rover onto the grass at the side of the road, a few hundred metres from Scabba Wath Bridge. On the left-hand side of the road was a dry-stone wall, with fields the other side going down to the river at the bottom of the dale. On the right was grass, moorland and some low bushes with yellow flowers. Sheep were wandering freely over the moorland, as they often do at this time of year. It was early evening, not yet dark, and a light rain was falling.

Scott and Neville got out of the Land Rover and climbed to a group of people standing further up the hillside. Kay Harding, the police doctor, was on her knees examining a man's body. He was lying on his stomach, his head turned away looking up the hillside.

Harding stood up as Neville and Scott arrived.

'One of us,' she said, looking at Neville.

Neville's eyes asked the question.

'Brian Barningham,' said Harding. 'He was an inspector in Leyburn. He stopped work last year just after his sixtieth birthday and moved to Richmond.'

'God!' Neville shook his head in disbelief. 'I know. I was there at his leaving party. I knew him quite well.'

Harding bent down to look at the body again.

'I'm afraid it's not pretty to look at,' she said. 'He was strangled. He was also hit in the face about the time he died.'

'Is it the same ...' began Scott.

'Yes,' replied Harding, straightening up and passing a plastic bag to Neville. Inside it was a playing card. The three of spades. And across the middle of the card were the words 'By hand'. Neville passed it to Scott, who looked at it and gave it back to Harding.

'But there is a difference,' said Harding, bending down again for another look. 'The body's been moved.'

'Killed here and just moved?' asked Scott. 'Or killed somewhere else and brought here?'

'Oh, killed somewhere else and brought here,' answered Harding. 'I mean, he's lying on his front now. But after death I'd say he spent a short time on his back and then longer on his side.'

Neville looked at the moorland round about, then down at the roadside.

'Get some scene-of-crime tape,' he said, turning to Scott. 'I want it twenty metres each side of the body, down to the road. No one else can walk there until that area's been searched.'

'Right,' replied Scott, nodding at a couple of the officers in the group to do what Neville wanted.

'And I mean "searched",' continued Neville. 'Carefully. I want officers on their hands and knees. The killer must have come by car, so look for tyre marks by the side of the road too.'

'OK,' answered Scott.

'Who found the body?' asked Neville.

'A local farmer,' replied Harding. 'First farm on the left, that way.' She pointed down the road to her right. 'He had to get back – said something about his sheep.'

'OK,' said Neville. 'We'll talk to him.'

'Time of death?' asked Scott.

'Some time this afternoon,' said Harding. 'Three or four, maybe. It was quite a warm afternoon before the rain came, so it's not easy to be exact.'

'OK. Thanks, Kay,' said Neville. 'He's all yours.'

'He was divorced,' said Neville, looking at Scott. 'But I guess someone ought to tell his ex. I'll go and do that. I know where she lives. You look after things here and talk to the farmer who found the body. I'll meet you back in Reeth in an hour or so.'

* * *

At seven o'clock the following morning, Fiona

Russell yawned as she checked her email in the operations room. She'd had three hours sleep. She'd stayed up well into the night reading reports from officers in Bristol, Richmond and Reeth. A new email had come in from Bristol overnight, but it didn't contain any useful information. She'd now seen everything to do with the first two murders and everything that had so far come in about the third. The only thing that seemed odd to her was that the third body had been moved. Why was that? Had he had to move it? And if so, why?

She was just turning these questions over in her mind when the door opened and Neville and Scott came into the room, carrying cups of coffee. Neville was speaking.

'... they're going to go crazy,' he was saying. 'Two murders in forty-eight hours.' He looked at Russell. 'Journalists!' he explained – with feeling. 'As if we didn't have better things to do than talk to them! We have work to do.'

Neville walked through to the interview room and put his coffee on the table.

'The killer's made a mistake,' he said, changing the subject. 'I'm sure of it. He's made a mistake and we've got to make the most of it.' He looked at Russell.

'What do you think about it, Fiona?' Neville asked. 'Moving the body, I mean.'

Russell joined them and they all sat down.

'It is strange,' she replied. She thought for a minute and then looked at Neville.

'Up until now we haven't looked at any CCTV film, have we?' she asked.

'There are no CCTV cameras where the bodies were found,' replied Neville. 'We've got no idea what to look for, or where.'

'We might have now,' said Russell.

'What do you mean?' asked Neville.

'Well, we now know Barningham was killed some time soon after three o'clock. And his body was found at about six thirty.' She put a finger to her lips as she continued to think her idea through. 'Our killer might live in one of the villages in Swaledale or Arkengarthdale, or Wensleydale even. But equally he might live in one of the nearby towns.'

'Where there are CCTV cameras,' said Scott.

'Good thinking,' said Neville. He looked at Scott. 'Get going, Helen. We want all CCTV film from the roads leading out here from both Richmond and Leyburn.'

'And Catterick?' asked Scott.

'Yes,' replied Neville. 'And maybe Barnard Castle too. Also, get someone to keep those journalists off our backs. I'll talk to them later this afternoon if I've got time.'

Scott got up and left the room.

'Any news from Bristol?' asked Neville, turning to Russell.

'It's still possible that Kenworthy and McFadyen knew each other,' answered Russell. 'We now know they were both at the university at the same time. However, the Bristol police haven't been able to establish that they ever actually met.'

'OK,' said Neville. 'Keep on at them. And what about McFadyen's husband? Any news on him?'

'He's in the clear,' replied Russell. 'Helen sent some officers round to talk to his neighbours. One of them saw him putting his rubbish out at the time of the murder.'

'Right,' said Neville. 'I suppose crossing someone off our list is a kind of move forward.'

Russell smiled tiredly at Neville as Scott came back into the room.

'This latest murder does raise a few questions,'

said Russell. 'The first is: why did he move the body this time? Also, the fact that Barningham was ex-police – is that important in any way?'

Neville and Scott both shook their heads.

'No idea,' replied Scott.

'The other thing,' continued Russell, 'is: why is he doing this? There has to be a reason, even if it only means something to him. Look at the ways he's killed: hit on the head with a stone, stabbed with a knife, strangled. The first card didn't have any writing on it. But the second and third said "By knife" and "By hand".'

'It's almost as if he's trying out different ways of killing people,' said Scott.

'Exactly,' replied Russell.

There was silence for a moment.

'Maybe to show that he can,' suggested Scott.

More silence.

'He doesn't seem to be getting pleasure from making people suffer,' said Russell. 'I mean, some serial killers take ages – they almost play with the people they kill.'

'So you'd say it's the act of killing that's important to him then, would you?' asked Neville.

'Yes, I think so,' replied Russell.

* * *

Later that morning Scott was walking back from the baker's in Silver Street, after an unsuccessful attempt to buy some cheese sandwiches, when she saw Jonathan Greene walk into the Shoulder of Mutton pub. He had a large bag over his shoulder and was wearing a patterned grey shirt and grey trousers. Given his appearance and build, it wasn't a great fashion choice. He looked a bit like a baby elephant.

'Well, there's always one way to find out what he's doing here,' Scott said to herself. She waited a couple of minutes and then walked into the pub after him.

Greene was sitting in the corner beside a coal fire. There was a glass of beer in front of him and he was reading the *Darlington and Stockton Times*. He looked up as Scott came over to his table.

'A little light reading,' he said with a smile. 'I love local newspapers.' From the way he spoke Scott realised he meant something quite different.

'Not good enough for you, the D and S?' asked Scott. 'Not in the same class as the nationals and the London dailies?'

'Hey, I was joking,' replied Greene, looking a little

hurt.

'Yeah, right,' said Scott, not believing him for a moment.

Scott pulled out a chair and sat down.

'I'd like to ask you a few questions,' she said.

Greene said nothing. Scott looked him straight in the eye.

'It would be very helpful if you'd answer them here and now,' she said, 'rather than make me take you to the operations room to talk to DI Neville. I think you'd prefer it too. In the inspector's judgement, journalists are the lowest form of human life. You may have noticed.'

Greene smiled.

'Ask away,' he said. 'I can't promise to answer them all. But I never mind talking to an attractive woman.'

Scott felt slightly sick at the thought of being chatted up by Greene, but she continued.

'As you know, we're looking into who could have your mobile number, especially up here in North Yorkshire,' she began, 'so it would be helpful for us to know why you're here.'

'Ah!' said Greene.

'We know you didn't come up here to report on

the murders,' said Scott.

'Ah!' said Greene again. He bit his bottom lip, then smiled and said, 'How badly do you want to know?'

Scott wasn't sure if this was a real question or a chat-up line. It didn't really matter to her.

'How badly do you want to see DI Neville?' she asked in reply, looking at Greene. Her eyes were stony.

Greene pushed a hand through what hair he had left.

'This is really difficult ...' he began. 'I mean, I don't tell anyone about my stories until—'

'Where were you earlier this year?' interrupted Scott. 'I understand you were out of the country for a time. Where did you go?'

Greene paused a moment, then seemed to accept that he would have to answer.

'The Middle East,' he said.

'The Gulf?' asked Scott.

'Yes.'

Scott had a sudden thought. The army. Catterick Garrison was about twenty kilometres from Reeth. There were over 12,000 soldiers there, all of whom had seen active service.

'The army,' she said.

'Yes,' said Greene.

'You've been talking to soldiers,' she said. It wasn't really a question.

'Yes,' said Greene.

'We haven't found any soldiers' numbers in your phone book,' said Scott.

'I told you. I don't keep many numbers in my phone book,' he answered.

'But you've given your number to some soldiers,' said Scott.

'Yes,' replied Greene.

Scott took out a notebook and pushed it across the table.

'I want the name of every soldier who has your number,' she said.

'But—'

'Now,' said Scott.

Greene held out his hands.

'I can give you some names,' he said, 'but not all of them. I meet a lot of these guys in pubs. We just chat. I don't ask them their names. Quite often they don't want me to know. With the kind of story I'm investigating, if their name gets in the paper, it makes trouble for them with the army. They have to be careful.'

Scott took out a pen and gave it to Greene. She looked him in the eye and said nothing. Greene pulled the notebook towards him and started writing.

'When you've done that,' said Scott, 'you can tell me exactly what you're investigating.'

Chapter 5
Caught on film

I got away with it – but I was exhausted! So tired that this morning I slept till midday. Part of the tiredness was physical – first the fight, then moving the body. Part of the tiredness was in the mind – because I hadn't been completely ready for this adventure. I'd had to think quickly. And carefully.

No one else was at home when I got up. I made a coffee and thought back to yesterday afternoon. I needed to check I had made no mistakes.

I had walked home for a blanket, a change of clothes and the three of spades. Although I was in a hurry, I walked – running would have drawn attention to me. I put the blanket, the card and a pair of binoculars in a bag, and went out to look for a car. Stealing a car is easy when you know how – and I know how.

I drove it back to my 'helper's' house and parked round the back, got the body onto the back seat and covered it with the blanket. Then I started out towards Reeth. On the way I thought about where to leave the body: a side road, somewhere quiet, where

I could get the body out without being seen. It was about four o'clock in the afternoon, but a light rain had been falling all afternoon. There wouldn't be many walkers out. I decided on the perfect place.

I drove along the Swaledale road and turned left over Scabba Wath Bridge. Then I turned left again onto the road back to Grinton and Reeth. There was moorland here with low bushes that would hide the body for a while. I pulled off the road – there was grass by the side of the road, so I wouldn't leave any tyre marks. Then I got out of the car and carefully checked the countryside around me with the binoculars. Nobody.

Working quickly, I got the body off the back seat. Holding it by the ankles, I pulled it up the side of the hill and hid it behind some bushes. I left the card in the man's hand, looked round to make sure there was nothing for the police to find, and made my way back to the car.

There was little else left to do – get rid of the car, change my clothes and burn the ones I was wearing, drop my shoes in the river. Easy!

It had all been rather hurried, and I was sorry about that. But now that it's over, I can relax, look back and enjoy the moment. I can put a third sticker on my murder map to show where the third body will be found – if it hasn't been found already.

I can also start planning my next adventure. I'm getting a taste for this. Not only can people see how powerful I am and what I can achieve, but I'm also enjoying the feeling. It's the high that comes with every kill, the certainty that it's right to be doing this.

The next one will be two. Double pleasure. I'll use the gun. I've been out on the moors and fired a couple of shots just to get used to it. There are only five shots left in the gun and I don't know if I can get any more bullets. Because of that, I want to get close so there's no chance of missing. I know when and where it's going to happen too. It will be in the early evening, at the roadside. So I'll need to steal another car – but that won't be a problem. Perhaps tonight is a bit early. Or perhaps not. Already I can feel the excitement building. Already I know how good the feeling will be.

Yes. Tonight.

* * *

That evening Fiona Russell was at her desk, wondering when she'd next get a good night's sleep. She reached for her coffee and heard another email come through on her computer: a report of two cars stolen in Richmond the afternoon before. Two stolen cars was pretty unusual for Richmond. It wasn't a big town. Cars didn't often get stolen and two on the same day was strange.

A dark green Mini had been stolen from the Market Square late in the evening and a silver Skoda had gone missing from the Gallowfields Business Park some time between 3:15 p.m. and 3:45 p.m. The Skoda had been stolen around the time of the third murder. So – a Skoda then. Maybe.

Russell made a note of the car number. Then she started up some CCTV film on her computer, film from the one camera in Richmond that covered the road out to Swaledale and Reeth. She pressed fast-forward until the time in the right-hand corner was 15:13:27. That was about the right time, but was it the right road? Of course, the car thief might not be the killer at all. He, or she, might not even have headed towards Swaledale.

Russell hit play. Cars went past. Then cars didn't go past. Then one car. Then no cars for a long time. It wasn't a busy road. She hit fast-forward, then play again when more traffic came along.

The time got to 16:00:00. The Little Red Bus went

past – the bus service from Richmond to Reeth and then on up Swaledale – then a farm vehicle followed by a line of cars, then nothing.

Russell stopped the film and went back. The cars

behind the farm vehicle were quite close together. She froze the picture and looked closely. At the back of the line was a BMW, then an Audi, a Ford, a Land Rover, but what was the first car? It was difficult to see. The CCTV was black and white so that was no help.

She zoomed in close and moved down the picture to try and see the car's back number plate. It was hidden – the Land Rover was too close. She went back a couple of minutes and started the film again. This time she played it slowly.

When the cars came into view she froze the film and zoomed in on the back of the first car. Yes! It was a Skoda – that was good. She let the film go forward again slowly. Stop! She could see half the number plate, just the last three letters. They were the same as the last letters of the stolen Skoda. Yes! That was very good!

Something like electricity rushed through her; her head felt light. The feeling almost took her breath away.

Just then Scott came into the room. There was an excited look on her face, but she stopped when she saw Russell.

'Fiona, are you OK?' she asked, looking worriedly

at the other woman.

Russell waved a hand and gave her a big smile.

'I'm fine, I'm fine,' she said. 'Come and look at this.'

She took the film back to where the line of cars first came into view.

'Watch this,' she said. 'The first car behind the tractor is the one to watch. I think our man is driving it.'

They watched the film closely until the cars went out of sight. The cars were moving away from the camera so it was impossible to see the drivers. Russell took the film back to the beginning and they watched it again slowly. Then Russell stopped the film and looked at Scott.

'Why do you think it's him?' asked Scott.

'The car was stolen around the time of the murder,' answered Russell.

'Ah,' said Scott. 'You think he stole a car rather than used his own – if he has one.'

'Yes,' replied Russell. She reached out and took hold of Scott's arm. 'If it's him, he stole the car,' she said. 'And he drove out from Richmond – so maybe he lives there.' She smiled at Scott. 'He's starting to make mistakes.'

Russell let go of Scott's arm and stood up.

'Anyway,' she said, 'you came in here with something important.'

'Oh yes,' said Scott, the excited look returning to her face. 'Let's find Charles. We need to compare notes.'

* * *

Half an hour later Neville, Scott and Russell were sitting round the table in the interview room.

'Let me get this straight,' said Neville, looking at Scott. 'The investigation that Jonathan Greene is working on at the moment is to do with the army.'

'Yes,' replied Scott. 'He's looking at the effects of active service on soldiers who have been out in the Middle East and the Gulf – mainly the effects on their minds, and what the government is doing to help soldiers who are badly affected.'

'I thought he was a crime reporter,' said Russell.

'He is,' replied Scott. 'He thinks the government isn't doing enough. Apparently he feels that their position can be seen as criminal. Greene's brother was a soldier. He was so badly affected that he had to leave the army. He now never goes out of his house. For Greene, this is personal.'

'I see,' said Neville. 'And you think a soldier sent Greene the text message about the cards – a soldier that Greene gave his number to.'

'That does seem logical,' said Russell. 'I mean, we think the killer lives locally. We think the killer sent the text message. The killer had Greene's mobile number. And the only people up here that he has given his mobile number to are soldiers and a few other journalists.'

'And how many soldiers did Greene give his number to?' Neville asked Scott.

'That's the problem,' replied Scott. 'He doesn't know. I've got half a dozen names here, but he's talked to lots more. Soldiers are quite happy to talk to him. But because his investigation is unlikely to be popular with the army, they're less happy about giving him their names.'

Neville looked at Russell.

'And you think you have the killer on CCTV in a stolen Skoda, leaving Richmond just after the last murder?'

'Yes,' replied Russell. 'I need to see if he comes back the same way later. I might even get to see him since he'll be facing the camera. But you know how clear CCTV pictures are. I don't expect to be able to tell you what he looks like.'

She opened her mouth to say something else, but then stopped and thought.

'Yes?' asked Neville.

'As far as I know,' said Russell slowly, still thinking her ideas through, 'no cars were stolen around the days of the first two murders. I'll check that, but I'm pretty sure I'm right.'

Neville and Scott said nothing. They waited for Russell to finish making her point.

'That means he must have used his own car to come out here for the first two murders,' said Russell.

'So more than likely he's going to be on CCTV in his own car on those days,' said Scott. 'If they still have the film.'

'They don't use videotapes these days,' said Russell. 'Everything's on computer – hard disk. And it's kept for longer, so we should be able to get hold of it.'

'Right,' said Neville, making a decision. 'Fiona, first check the CCTV to see if you've got him coming back into Richmond yesterday. Then look at the film from the same camera for the first two murders.'

He turned to Scott.

'Helen,' he said, 'you follow up the army idea. You've got the list of soldiers. Go over to Catterick.

Talk to them. Ask questions. See if you can find out who else talked to Greene. Take a couple of officers with you. This could be important.'

Pushing his fingers through his hair, Neville stood up.

'It'll be good to have something new to tell the journalists tomorrow,' he said. 'I have to say I'm getting sick of seeing my photo on the front page of national newspapers.'

* * *

As Neville, Scott and Russell were making their way back into the operations room, they heard a woman police officer talking on the phone.

'Yes,' she said. 'Yes, I agree that's very strange. Well, I'll tell my boss and ...' At that moment she looked round and saw Neville behind her. 'Just a moment. My boss is right here. I'll pass you over.'

Neville raised his eyebrows.

'Inspector Atkins from Richmond. Something about a stolen car,' said the officer.

Neville took the phone.

'DI Neville,' he said. He lifted a hand to tell Scott and Russell to wait. They heard his end of the conversation.

'That's right ... Yes, I know. We've just been talking about it ... Yes, that is strange ... Yes, well, I'd like forensics to examine it as soon as possible. We think it may have been used by the killer ... OK, I'll leave it with you ... Tell them to ring me as soon as they have anything.'

Neville gave the phone back to the officer and looked at Scott and Russell.

'They found the car in almost exactly the same place it was stolen from,' he told them. 'Atkins is getting forensics on to it.'

'Strange to be in the same place,' said Scott.

Russell looked thoughtful. 'I wonder why?' she asked.

'What do you mean?' asked Neville.

'Why did he put it back in the same place?' she asked. 'There must be a reason. It could be close to where he lives – so it was easy to get to. Or it could be a long way from where he lives to make life difficult for us.'

Scott walked over to the door and back, thinking. The others watched her.

'The timing,' she said. 'The timing is important. We know the time of death: soon after three. By four o'clock we've got him on the CCTV camera coming out of Richmond.'

'Exactly,' replied Russell.

'He must have stolen the car from somewhere close to the scene of the crime,' said Scott.

'The car was in the Gallowfields Business Park,' said Russell.

'Not far from Barningham's house,' added Scott.

'Which might be the scene of the crime,' said Neville, 'although we haven't found any signs there.'

Just then a phone rang on the other side of the operations room.

A police officer answered it, then looked at Neville.

'Another one, sir,' he said. 'In fact, this time there are two.'

The room went silent. Russell's eyes opened wide. Neville went across the room and took the phone. After a short conversation he put the phone down and turned to face the room.

'The four and five of spades. By gun,' he said. 'He's shot a young couple out by Surrender Bridge.'

He looked at Scott.

'Let's go,' he said.

'Sir?' asked Russell. She knew they normally used

first names, but she was intending to ask for something special. A little extra politeness would be good politics.

Neville looked at her. She could see he knew what the question was. She could also see what the answer would be.

'Yes,' he replied.

'I know the scene of the crime isn't where I'm usually supposed to be ...' she began.

'Yes, yes, come on,' replied Neville. 'Get your coat and come with us. But don't be sick.'

'I have seen dead bodies before,' said Russell.

Chapter 6
Closing in

Life just gets better and better. Or is it death that's getting better? Anyway, it was another perfect killing. I'm so good at it. Why they didn't want me, I just don't understand.

I walked down to the old station to find myself a car. The old railway station is now a cinema and there's a car park in front of it. If the owner of the car was watching a film, I might even get the car back before the film finished. He or she wouldn't even know it had been stolen. It would all depend how the evening went.

It was early evening, not dark yet. You might think I was taking chances, stealing cars in broad daylight. But I'm quick. I broke into the car quite easily, put my gun on the floor in front of the passenger seat and got the car started. Then I drove out towards Reeth and Swaledale. I knew what I was looking for – there are small parking areas beside the road in a number of places in the dale. I would drive round until I found one with a car parked in it: maybe an old couple who'd stopped to look at the view or some young lovers having a kiss and a cuddle. It's all the same to me. I just want to show what I can do.

I got to Reeth first. The lights were on in Reeth Memorial Hall. I'd read in the papers that the police were using it as an operations room. It seemed funny to be driving past the place they were trying to catch me from. 'Catch me if you can,' I thought. 'But you can't. You won't.'

There was no one parked between Reeth and Langthwaite, so I turned left along the road to Surrender Bridge and headed towards Swaledale.

There's a ford along here, where a stream goes over the road and you have to drive through the water. The ford is famous because it was always shown at the beginning of a popular TV series about a vet. I'd watched those programmes as a kid, but these days I only watch crime shows.

From there I drove on to Surrender Bridge. As I came over the top of the hill and looked down towards the bridge, I could see that, just over the other side, a blue car was parked and there were people in it. Two people. Just what I was looking for.

I drove over the bridge and then stopped – but not too close to the other car. I didn't want to alarm them. When I'd stolen the car I'd noticed that there was a map on the back seat. I thought I'd try the map business again.

I put the gun in my pocket and opened the map. Then I got out and walked across.

There was a young couple in the car. He was about twenty, dark-haired, good-looking; she was the same age, blonde and pretty. They had been kissing, but had broken off when I stopped my car.

Seeing me coming towards them, map in hand, the young woman opened the driver's window.

'Can I help you?' She smiled at me.

I was only a couple of metres away by then. I smiled back, took out my gun and shot her in the head. She fell forward onto the wheel.

Her boyfriend shouted something, but he didn't have time to do anything. I pointed the gun a few centimetres to the left and shot him through the head as well.

I checked they were both dead and then sat both the bodies up in their seats so they looked alive. Finally I reached into the car and threw the four and five of spades onto the back seat.

When you fire a gun like this, the bullet shoots out of the front of the gun and the casing, which holds the bullet, is thrown out of the side, sometimes a few metres away. One casing was easy to find. I picked it up and put it in my pocket. The other was nowhere to be seen. I searched for it among the grass and small bushes, but I just couldn't find it.

After a few minutes I heard the sound of a car in the distance. It was time to go. Even if the police found the casing, it was unlikely to matter. Taking the casings was just me being careful, leaving nothing to chance. What the police really needed was the gun. With the gun and the bullets they could get a match. But they would never find the gun.

I got back in my car and drove away.

It would be some time before the bodies were found. Nobody would think twice about gunshots out here. Farmers are always shooting rabbits, and the rich pay large amounts of money to come and shoot birds. The sound of gunshots isn't unusual in the Dales.

I drove back to Richmond enjoying the moment, feeling the excitement run through my body and already looking forward to the next killing. I'm getting closer to my goal.

* * *

It took Neville, Scott and Russell fifteen minutes

to reach Surrender Bridge from the operations room in Reeth. Neville and Russell went in a police Land Rover; Scott took her own car. Black and yellow scene-of-crime tape was already closing off a wide area around a small blue car. Two police Land Rovers were parked on the opposite side of the road behind a red Toyota 4x4. A man and a woman police officer were talking to someone in the Toyota. A third police officer was setting up some large lights so that everyone could see what was going on. A fourth was standing just near the scene-of-crime tape.

'The police doctor's on her way,' he said as Neville came up to him.

Neville nodded towards the Toyota.

'What's happening there?' he asked.

'The young woman's mother,' replied the officer. 'Her daughter was out with her boyfriend and said she'd be home for dinner by eight. When she wasn't back by ten thirty, her mum came out looking for her. She said she knows the places they usually go. We've been trying to calm her down, but understandably she's really upset.'

'Husband?' asked Neville.

'A couple of the guys have gone to get him, and to

tell the boy's parents,' replied the officer.

'The cards?' asked Neville.

'On the back seat,' replied the officer. 'I haven't touched anything. As soon as I saw the bodies and the cards, I closed the area off.'

'Good. Thank you.' Neville turned to Scott. 'Let's have a look.'

They took some white plastic overshoes out of the back of the Land Rover and put them over their own shoes. Then they bent under the police tape and slowly and carefully walked over to the blue car.

'What do you think?' asked Neville and they walked round the car looking in through the windows.

'I'd say they were shot from fairly close,' said Scott. 'But I guess we should wait and see what Kay has to say.'

Just then a green Land Rover arrived and Kay Harding got out. She immediately put on overshoes and joined Scott and Neville. She reached in through the car window and felt the necks of both the young people for signs of life.

'No surprises there,' she said. 'But I have to check.'

Then she bent down and looked at the bullet holes in their heads.

'They were shot from less than a metre away,' she

said. 'Let me get on with things and I'll tell you more when I've finished here. I realise how important this is.'

'Thanks, Kay,' said Neville.

Neville and Scott made their way back outside the police tape, where Russell joined them.

'Charles?' she began.

Neville looked at her in reply.

'If he came from Richmond again ...' She left the sentence unfinished.

'Good thinking,' said Neville, looking at his watch. 'Let's say he took some time to find what he was looking for. So first see if there are any reports of stolen cars. Then check CCTV film from about six o'clock to eleven o'clock. You know what to look for.'

* * *

Russell had a busy night. To start with, no cars had yet been reported stolen. The next problem was that CCTV cameras in North Yorkshire weren't managed by the police, but by a local government officer. He wasn't happy to get a midnight phone call from Fiona Russell wanting CCTV film from that evening and from two weeks earlier.

'Can't it wait until morning?' he complained sleepily.

'Sure,' replied Russell. 'I'll suggest that to my boss.

I'm sure he'd be happy for you to come into the police station until then. Helping us with our inquiries. Through the night.'

'God!' thought Russell, smiling to herself. 'I've spent so long with police officers I'm starting to sound like one.'

Russell received the film by email within the hour and started work. First she played through the film from the evening before, noting the number of each car or van that went from Richmond towards Reeth and Swaledale. Then she went through again noting cars going back into Richmond. Then she matched the two lists. Ten cars were on both lists. She yawned, pushed her fingers through her hair and looked across the operations room. Neville and Scott had returned at two in the morning. They were in the interview room working their way through a pile of papers.

Russell poured herself a coffee from the machine by the window and went back to her computer. There was no point telling Neville anything until she had names and addresses for the owners of those ten cars. In any case, she felt sure the killer had used a stolen car.

After half an hour on the Driver and Vehicle Database, Russell had the information she needed.

She went over to join Neville and Scott in the interview room. They looked up as she came in.

'Ten names and addresses,' she said, putting a piece of paper on the table. 'Owners of cars that left Richmond early yesterday evening in the direction of Reeth and returned some time later. They're all possibles. But my guess is the car was stolen, even though it hasn't yet been reported. Anyway, I'll start on the film from the first two murders now.'

Just then the phone rang. Neville picked up.

'DI Neville.' He listened for a moment then said, 'Just a moment, Kay. Helen and Fiona are here. I'll put you on speakerphone.'

He pressed a button and Kay Harding's voice came into the room loud and clear.

'You owe me, Charles,' she said. 'I've been working through the night on this one for you.'

'Noted,' replied Neville. 'What have you got?'

'I can narrow the time of death to between eight and nine thirty, if that helps,' she answered.

'It might,' replied Neville.

'They were both young and healthy. Both, as you know, died from a bullet wound to the head,' continued Harding.

'OK,' said Neville. 'And the bullets?'

'Yes, the bullets,' said Harding. 'Both from the same gun. Both nine-millimetre. Both made in Iraq.'

'What?' Neville half-shouted the question. 'What do you mean?'

'Your guys found a casing from one of the bullets at the scene of the crime,' explained Harding. 'There was some writing on it. I copied it and emailed it to a friend of mine at Newcastle University. He's a lecturer in Middle Eastern Studies. He told me that the writing was Arabic and that it says "Al-Qādisiyyah". I looked it up on the internet.'

'And?' asked Neville.

'Al-Qādisiyyah is a province in southern Iraq,' said Harding, 'but it's also the name of a factory that makes a nine-millimetre gun called a Tariq – basically a Beretta M1951, but made in Iraq. They've been making them since before 1990 and they're still used today by the Iraqi police.'

'The Iraqi police!' There was disbelief in Neville's voice.

Russell put a hand on his arm.

'No,' she said. 'It adds up. It's all to do with the army. Soldiers out in Iraq or Afghanistan, or wherever, they get lots of opportunities to get their hands on guns, bullets, knives, all sorts of things – especially from the people they are fighting.'

'Thanks very much, Kay,' said Neville, switching the phone off, deep in thought. He turned to Russell.

'So you're saying,' he said, 'that it's easy for a soldier to get hold of a Tariq nine-millimetre and bring it back to Britain, as a kind of war prize.'

'Absolutely,' said Russell. 'I worked on a case in London a few years ago where an ex-soldier was selling guns to criminals – guns that he'd brought back from places all around the world.'

Nobody spoke for a moment.

'We come back to soldiers and the army again,' said Neville. He looked at Scott. 'How are you getting on with Greene's list?' he asked.

'I called Catterick earlier,' she said. 'There were six names on Greene's list. Of those, three were at the garrison at the time of the first two murders. And the other three have recently gone out to Afghanistan. They left before the murders started. However, I did manage to speak to one of the first three soldiers. He's given me the names of nine others who spoke to Greene, but didn't tell him who they were.'

Scott looked at Neville and Russell.

'But don't get too excited,' she warned them. 'I get the feeling Greene spoke to a lot more people.'

'Never mind that,' said Neville. 'It's a start. As Fiona said at the beginning, we only need to get lucky once.'

'I don't suppose you found out which of those nine live in Richmond, did you?' asked Russell. 'That's where the cars have been stolen from.'

Scott started to look through the papers on the table in front of her and pulled out the one she was looking for.

'Yes,' she replied, 'I did.' She looked at the list. 'Two of them.'

She turned the paper round so that the others could read it.

'I'll look on the Driver and Vehicle Database to see if either of them has a car,' said Russell. 'Then if we look at the CCTV from the days of the first two murders, we might find a match.'

'Do it,' said Neville and he looked at Scott. 'And, Helen, give Fiona a hand. I've got a feeling we might be getting close.'

* * *

Ten minutes later Russell gave Scott a piece of

paper with letters and numbers written on it.

'Two car numbers,' she said. 'One for each of the soldiers who live in Richmond. I've emailed the CCTV film from the day of the second murder to your computer. You look through that. I'll look at the first one.'

'You were right about a car being stolen last night,' said Scott as she sat down. 'It was reported at ten twenty last night in Richmond. The report's only just made it onto the computer.'

Russell thought for a moment.

'Has the car been found yet?' she asked.

'I don't think so,' replied Scott.

'Tell them to try the Gallowfields Business Park,' said Russell.

When Scott looked questioningly at her, Russell said, 'Just a guess.'

Then she pushed her fingers through her hair and took a deep breath. She looked at the two names and addresses on the paper in front of Scott.

'I don't know Richmond that well,' she said. 'Is either of these addresses near the Business Park?'

'Neither of them is very far away,' answered Scott.

Russell sat down in front of her computer. She put

her elbows on the table and rested her chin on her hands. She thought for a few moments.

'I think,' she began, speaking slowly. 'I think that the third murder – the one where he first stole a car – I think that maybe it wasn't planned as well as the others. I think he was surprised in some way.'

Scott looked at Russell.

'I also think,' continued Russell, 'that he felt he had to move the body in a hurry. And that first stolen car was taken from the Business Park because it's close to where he lives. Leaving the car there when he'd finished with it was just an attempt to confuse us.'

'That sounds a reasonable guess to me,' replied Scott.

'OK,' said Russell, having another look at the car numbers in front of her. 'Let's see if we can find one of these two.'

Russell and Scott started watching the different films on their computers.

Forty-five minutes later Russell watched the same thirty seconds of film for the third time. Then she sat back in her chair.

'Got you,' she said quietly.

Chapter 7
The Reid family

After the shooting I wanted to put the car back in the station car park. But as I got near, I could see a police car, and a man and a woman talking to two police officers. I drove by quickly, before they saw me. Then I went up to the Gallowfields Business Park. If I leave all the stolen cars in the same place, the police won't know what to think.

I walked home, thinking about the shooting. It was cleverly done in my opinion: a foreign gun, a stolen car, two clean kills. Two killings nearer my goal. I'm like a well-oiled machine, a well-oiled killing machine. Training – ha! I don't need training for this. This is all down to planning, organisation and being brave enough to believe I can do it. Being brave – that's it. They never really thought I was brave enough.

Before I went home, I turned down a side street and decided to keep walking. I didn't want to arrive home and have to talk to anyone. Also I had to put the gun back in its hiding place. I would stay out for another half an hour until everyone at home had gone to bed.

While I walked I could plan my next adventure. It should be soon. Maybe even tomorrow. The sooner I reach my goal, my target number, the sooner I can show the world what I'm made of, and the sooner they'll want me.

Tomorrow, then. Tomorrow morning. A drowning, I think. There are plenty of paths by the river in both Swaledale and Arkengarthdale. It should be easy to surprise someone, hold them under the water and feel the life leave their body. Of course, they would fight back, but I would be prepared for this. I could either knock them out first and then hold them under. Or I could choose someone smaller and less powerful than me. I considered both courses of action. I liked them both. I would decide tomorrow.

And where do I plan to do this? Mentally I worked my way along the River Swale from Reeth to the upper dale. There's a favourite place of mine where a stream called Barney Beck joins the river. I had many picnics there as a child; I've walked that path many times as an adult; I know the place better than the back of my hand.

It was ten past eleven when I let myself quietly in through the front door. I stopped inside the door and listened. Silence. Gently I locked the door and went into the kitchen. From there a door leads through to the garage.

The garage is full of everything that we don't want in the house: old boxes, a clothes dryer, two bikes, a television that doesn't work, suitcases, all sorts of rubbish. The suitcases are kept on a kind of platform under the roof. I climbed up and opened one of them. Inside was a metal box. And in the metal box was a piece of material. I took the gun out of my pocket, put the material round the gun, the gun in the box, and the box back in the suitcase. That's where he keeps the gun – but he doesn't know that I know!

I'll put a sticker on my map tonight for tomorrow's adventure. You may think that's overconfident of me. But I don't think so. I know I won't fail.

* * *

'Major Alan Reid,' said Fiona Russell, writing on a piece of paper, 'owns a red Ford Focus, KV06EUU. I've got the car driving out of Richmond towards Swaledale at five twenty-five on the morning of the first murder and then back into Richmond at eleven forty.'

Helen Scott looked down her list of car numbers.

'I've got the same car at four thirty in the afternoon on the day of the second murder,' she said.

'We've got a match, Charles,' Russell called to Neville.

Neville came over to Russell's desk.

'Address?' he asked.

Russell gave him the piece of paper she had been writing on.

'Quarry Road, Richmond. Is that near the Gallowfields Business Park?' she asked.

'Very close,' said Neville. He looked at Scott. 'Come on, let's go,' he said. He turned to Russell. 'You too. I want to know what you think.'

Half an hour later, at seven thirty in the morning, Scott stopped the police car outside a smart-looking stone house on Quarry Road. The front garden was tidy and well kept. There was no red Ford Focus on the drive in front of the house, nor in the street. Neville, Scott and Russell went to the front door. Neville rang the bell.

There was the sound of someone coming to the door and then the door being unlocked. The door was opened by a white-haired woman in her sixties, wearing a dressing gown over her nightclothes.

'Yes?' she asked.

Neville held up his police ID.

'DI Neville, North Yorkshire Police,' he said. 'This is DS Scott and this is Ms Russell, a police analyst. We're looking for a Major Alan Reid.'

The woman looked worried.

'Alan?' she asked. 'What do you want him for?'

'I'm afraid I can't tell you that,' said Neville. 'Perhaps we could come in.'

The woman opened the door wider.

'Well, yes,' she said. 'I suppose you'd better. Come into the front room and I'll go and get Alan.'

The woman showed Neville, Scott and Russell into a bright room at the front of the house. They stood and looked round it: comfortable furniture, pictures of the dales, family photos, a grandfather clock in the corner.

'Alan!' They heard the woman shout upstairs. 'There are some police officers here to see you. You are OK coming down on your own?'

'I'm fine, Mum,' was the reply.

There was the sound of someone slowly coming downstairs. Then the door opened. The woman came back into the room followed by a man in his early thirties moving very slowly. Under each arm was a crutch to help him walk. His right leg was normal. His left leg was missing, the trouser leg cut off above the knee.

He looked round the room.

'You'll excuse me if I sit down,' he said. He made his way to a brightly coloured armchair, dropped into it and laid his crutches on the floor beside it.

'Roadside bomb. Afghanistan,' he said by way of explanation. 'I was the lucky one. It killed two of my men. I'm waiting for a new leg.'

Neville, Scott and Russell looked at each other. This man obviously wasn't their killer.

'What can I do for you?' asked Reid, looking at Neville.

'You're Major Alan Reid,' said Neville.

'Yes.'

'You own a red Ford Focus,' said Neville.

'Yes.'

'Where is it?' asked Neville.

'Isn't it in front of the house?' asked Reid.

'No, it isn't,' said Neville.

'Well, Terry's probably gone out in it,' replied Reid.

'Terry?' asked Neville.

'My brother,' explained Reid.

Russell noticed a photo on a small table beside her. Two young men and an older woman: Alan and Terry Reid and their mother. She picked the photo up and passed it to Neville.

'Is your brother in the army too?' asked Neville, looking at the photo.

'No, he's a gardener. Part-time. He works for a few people in different parts of Richmond,' answered Reid.

'Have you been to Iraq as well as Afghanistan?' asked Neville.

'Yes,' replied Reid. 'Twice.'

'Do you own a gun?' asked Scott.

'No,' replied Reid. 'Obviously I know how to shoot one. And I have one with me when I'm on active service. But when we're back home we're not allowed to take guns out of Catterick Garrison.'

There was a short silence.

'What about a Tariq nine-millimetre?' asked Scott.

'What do you mean?' asked Reid.

'I mean, something you brought home to remind you of your time in Iraq. A war prize,' said Scott.

'Major Reid,' said Neville, before Reid had time to answer, 'we're investigating the series of murders in the Dales. You will have read about them in the papers and seen the news reports. I expect an honest answer from you.'

Reid took a deep breath.

'Yes,' he said. 'I do have a Tariq nine-millimetre. But so, I'm sure, do a few hundred other soldiers and ex-soldiers. Mine is well hidden and hasn't been used since I brought it back.'

'Where is it?' asked Neville. 'We'd like to see it.'

Reid picked up his crutches and with difficulty stood up.

'I'll show you,' he said.

Neville nodded at Scott and she followed Reid out of the room.

During the conversation Russell had been looking round the room. She'd noticed more family photos and started to take a closer interest in them: a baby, a young boy and their parents; two teenage boys; two young men and their mother; a younger Alan Reid in army uniform. In fact there were three or four of Reid in uniform, but no recent photos of his brother.

Russell looked at Reid's mother, who had been sitting on the sofa, but taking no part in the conversation.

'Mrs Reid,' she began, 'is Terry younger than Alan?'

'Yes,' answered Mrs Reid. 'There's four years between them.'

'And did Terry want to join the army too?' asked Russell.

'Oh yes,' answered Mrs Reid. 'Once Alan was in the army, it was all Terry talked about – how they'd be in the army together. He always wanted to do what Alan did. You know, he looked up to him like younger brothers often do.'

'So what happened?' asked Russell.

'Well, he started the training,' said Mrs Reid, looking down at the floor, 'and then the army decided they didn't want him.'

Russell said nothing. She just looked questioningly at Mrs Reid.

Eventually the white-haired woman looked up at Russell.

'They said it was something to do with his mind. Something psychological,' she said. 'I didn't really understand it. He's healthy. Strong. He passed all the physical tests. He passed all the exams. And then they said he was "unsuited to life in the modern army".'

'How did he feel about that?' asked Russell.

'Well, you can imagine,' said Mrs Reid. 'Joining the army had been his life's ambition. His dream. And it just disappeared overnight. It was terrible for him. He was very, very disappointed – more than disappointed, actually. Angry, as well.'

Russell looked at Neville and then back at Mrs Reid.

'Do you think it changed him at all?' she asked. 'Not getting into the army.'

Mrs Reid thought about this for a moment.

'Yes,' she said. 'I think it did really. He used to be more open, more friendly with people. He's more private now. He's kind of turned in on himself.'

Just then the door of the front room opened and Scott came back into the room, Reid behind her. There was a gun in Scott's hand.

'A Tariq nine-millimetre,' she said. 'And it's been used recently.'

Mrs Reid made a sound and her hand went to her mouth.

'You can't think ...' she began. But she couldn't finish.

Reid's face was white. He looked shaken.

'It can't be Terry,' he said. 'He doesn't know I've got the gun. I've never told him about it. He's not ...' He too found himself lost for words.

'We'd like to look in his room,' said Neville.

'Of course,' said Mrs Reid, her voice shaky. 'It's at the top of the stairs on the right.'

Neville gave Scott a sign that she should stay with

the Reids. Then he and Russell headed up the stairs.

'We need to find him as soon as possible,' said Russell, as she climbed the stairs behind Neville. 'I think he's gone out to kill again.'

'Today?' said Neville.

'Yes,' replied Russell. 'Today. As a rule, once serial killers get started, the time between the killings gets shorter and shorter. It becomes like a drug. They need it more and more.'

Terry Reid's room was unnaturally tidy: a perfectly made bed, chair and desk arranged with mathematical neatness, pens and pencils in a line, bookshelves with books arranged in order of size, a clothes cupboard.

Neville opened the cupboard door. Russell started on the desk drawers. Two minutes later she was opening out a map she'd found in the third drawer down.

'Here,' she said. Neville came across to look.

'Look where the blue stickers are,' said Russell, pointing at the map. 'The first murder. The second. The third. The fourth and fifth.' Each sticker was at the place where one of the murders had happened.

'And an extra one here,' said Neville, pointing at another. 'Barney Beck. That must be where he's gone.'

Chapter 8

Catching the killer

I left the house early this morning. It was cloudy, but it looked as though the sky would clear later. I took Alan's car today. I don't want to steal a car too often. The science is so good these days you can never tell what the police might be able to find. I drove to Reeth and parked in the middle of the village. Then I started out towards the little stream called Barney Beck. The path goes across the fields down to the River Swale, then along the river bank, through some trees.

Just before Barney Beck, the path moves in closer to the river. There's a dry-stone wall on the right of the path and the river is just a couple of metres to the left, with tall trees growing on both banks. So here I am now at the place where Barney Beck joins the river. Waiting.

It's a private place. That's why I've chosen it. And because there are stepping stones across the stream.

Mum often brought Alan and me here when we were young. We'd walk from Reeth and stop here for a picnic and throw stones in the water. Then we'd either return the way we'd come or, when we were older, we'd walk on to Scabba Wath Bridge and back to Reeth on the other side of the river. Happy days.

My dad died when I was eighteen months old, so I didn't know him at all. Alan hardly remembers him either. Mum brought us up on her own. I always felt I was her favourite even though she was very fair. Alan was always out with his friends playing football or cycling or rock climbing or ... doing something. I spent a lot of time with Mum. We've always been very close.

I look both ways up and down the river. No one is coming yet. I find a place where I can hide behind the wall. If a couple or a group of walkers come past, I'll hide. I'm waiting for someone on their own.

Although I'm Mum's favourite, I've always been jealous of Alan. He's the successful one out of us. Mum was so pleased when he got into the army. I knew that I had to try too.

I look both ways again. I can see a group of four people in the distance coming along the path from Reeth. Quickly I get into my hiding place. It takes the group fifteen minutes to arrive and go past. I give them another five minutes to get well away. Then I come out for another look in both directions. No one.

Everything went well when I started my army training. There was nothing physically wrong with me. I passed my exams. Actually, I passed them well. But then there were psychological tests: questions which didn't seem to have a right or wrong answer; questions about being on active service, about being on the front line. And then they told me I was unsuitable. At first I couldn't believe it. Being a soldier was the only thing I wanted. The army had refused me – how would I be able to look at myself in the mirror every morning? I did the only thing I could. I decided to show them they were wrong.

I look both ways along the river again. There's something red about a hundred metres away. I look through my binoculars. It's a woman in a red anorak. She's coming along the path from Scabba Wath. She's on her own.

I stretch my hands open and closed.

This is it.

I'm ready.

* * *

Scott drove. Neville and Russell sat in the back of the car. Neville took out his phone and made a call. Russell listened to him giving instructions for a minute, then reached forward and took a map off the front seat. She knew where Barney Beck was – along the River Swale between Reeth and Healaugh – she had walked there many times herself. But she wasn't sure of the easiest way to get to it. She opened the map.

From what Neville was saying on the phone it was clear to Russell that he knew the area well. She stopped listening as she looked at the map. The path from Reeth to where they thought Terry Reid might be was a long one. It would be quicker to park on the road just outside Healaugh and walk down through two fields. She was about to point this out to Neville when she heard him say, 'I want three men, armed, waiting in Reeth, in a car not a Land Rover. We'll pick them up as we go through. The closest we can get to Barney Beck is the road just outside Healaugh. Then we'll go on foot from there.' He turned off his phone.

Russell looked at Neville. His face looked tired, exhausted even, but now there was the light of excitement in his eyes as they closed in on their man. It had been like this with the other serial killer investigations she had worked on. The killings got closer and closer together in time; the police worked longer and longer hours, looking at more and more information; and then everything seemed to explode into madness towards the end.

Scott had the blue light going and made it from Richmond to Reeth in seventeen minutes. An unmarked police car was waiting opposite the Buck Hotel. She stopped beside it and Neville opened his window.

'Follow us,' he told the driver.

Five minutes later they pulled as far into the side of the road as they could, just outside the village of Healaugh. Russell realised why Neville had asked for a car, not a Land Rover. The Land Rover was a high vehicle and you'd be able to see the roof from down by the river, over the top of the dry-stone walls. Clever.

The police officers and Russell got out of the cars. Guns were handed to Neville and Scott. Neville looked at Russell.

'You stay here,' he said. 'You're not police. I don't want you anywhere near this.'

'No problem,' she said. She hoped that with her help Neville and Scott had got to the right place in time to save someone's life. But she was quite happy not to get any closer than this to a serial killer.

* * *

Scott opened the gate and the five officers entered

the field. She closed the gate. There were a few sheep on the far side of the field and, even with a killer running free, the farmer wouldn't be happy if they got out.

Quickly the officers made their way across the field, keeping low so that they wouldn't be seen. At the bottom of the field was another gate. Opening and closing it quietly, they ran across the next field to the wall at the bottom. They stayed low when they reached the wall. Scott looked round. Faces were set, lips pressed together, guns at the ready.

Neville nodded at Scott. She looked over the wall. It took her five seconds to realise what was happening. There were stepping stones across Barney Beck. A man was standing on one side of the stream. His back was towards her, but she was sure that it was Terry Reid. On the other side of the stream was a walker, a woman in a red anorak. She was a few metres away from the stepping stones and walking towards them. Reid put out a hand to help her over the stones. She took the offered hand. As she did so, she looked up and saw Scott.

Reid realised there was someone behind him. He turned suddenly and looked straight at Scott.

There was no time to think about what to do next. Scott lifted her gun over the wall and pointed it at Reid.

'Police!' she called. 'Let go of that woman's hand and don't move.'

Reid moved fast. He stepped quickly across the stream towards the woman, pulling the hand he was holding up behind her back and putting his other arm round her neck.

'Stay there,' he called to Scott. 'Don't come any closer.'

Scott knew that Neville could hear the conversation. Whispering and pointing, he would be sending the other officers to come up on Reid from behind – probably one to cross the river further back towards Reeth; the other two to go back up towards the road and to get behind Reid that way. She knew he'd stay hidden behind the wall.

'Don't do anything stupid,' said Scott. 'Just let her go and we'll talk.'

'Ha!' Reid laughed and started to move backwards. There was a wall and an opening into a field behind him. Scott could see what he was trying to do, but there was little she could do to stop him.

Suddenly Reid picked a stone off the top of the wall and hit the woman over the head with it. As she fell, he turned and ran fast up the field.

'Quick,' shouted Scott to Neville and the others, as she ran across the stepping stones to the injured woman. 'He's getting away. Towards the road.' Neville turned and started running.

* * *

At first Fiona Russell sat in the car, but it soon grew too warm in the autumn sunshine. She got out and stood by the gate that Neville, Scott and the others had first gone through. Her elbows were resting on the top of the gate and she was looking down towards the river. There had been some shouting a few minutes ago, but no shots. She wondered if they'd found Reid or not. A couple of minutes later she saw two of the officers from Reeth climbing over the dry-stone wall down the right-hand side of the field. It looked as if they'd certainly found someone.

She was about to go back to the car when she felt something hard stick into her back.

'Be very careful,' said a voice. 'This is a gun. And I don't want to use it.'

Russell felt sweat break out all over her body.

'What do you want?' she said. She knew it was Reid.

'Are the keys in the car?' asked Reid.

'I think so.'

'Open the passenger door and get in very slowly,' he said.

Russell turned a little to reach the car door. She couldn't see the gun, but she could feel it pressed hard into her side.

Out of the corner of her eye she could see him, the man she had been hunting. He was tall. He looked tired. He had small eyes, a weak chin and straight black hair.

'Take it easy,' she said. 'I'm not a police officer. But I can help you.'

'Don't talk,' he replied. 'Just move very slowly and get in the car.'

Gently, Russell let herself down onto the passenger seat. Reid kept the gun tight against her side.

'Now move across to the driver's seat,' ordered Reid.

Russell was about to move over when she heard a noise. She looked to her left. Neville and Scott had appeared at the gate into the field, guns in hands.

'Leave her alone,' said Neville, his gun pointing at Reid. 'Step back very slowly or we'll shoot.'

'I'll shoot too,' said Reid. 'I'm sure you don't want

this woman to die.'

Russell saw Neville and Scott look at each other.

'Where did you get the gun, Reid?' asked Scott. She stared at Reid, then she turned and her eyes met Russell's.

'Fiona, has he really got a gun?' she asked.

Russell thought quickly. She'd felt the gun, but she hadn't seen it. It wasn't the Tariq-nine millimetre – they'd seen that in his house earlier that morning. Did he have another gun? Should she take a chance? She turned sideways and pushed Reid hard in the chest with both hands. He fell away from the car onto his back. In his hand was a piece of wood that he had been pretending was a gun.

Within seconds Neville and Scott were through the gate. Neville pressed his gun to the side of Reid's head; Scott pulled his arms roughly behind his back and put the handcuffs on.

Reid started to fight against the handcuffs.

'Let me go!' he shouted, turning his head from side to side. 'I need to finish this. I need to reach my goal. I need to show them what I can do.'

Neville, Scott and Reid looked at each other.

'The army,' continued Reid, still trying to get his

hands free. 'I need to show them I've got what it takes. I need to show them I can kill people. And that I'm good at it. I need to show them I'm just the sort of person they want.'

Neville just shook his head.

* * *

Later that afternoon Neville, Scott and Russell were in the bar at the Half Moon Hotel. Reeth Memorial Hall had been emptied of all the desks, chairs, computers and phones that the police had brought. Terry Reid had been interviewed, taken to Richmond police station and would be interviewed again later. Helen Scott had been to Richmond to talk again to Reid's mother and brother. She had then returned to Reeth. Neville had spoken to the journalists and been interviewed for TV and radio.

Neville carried three glasses from the bar and put them on the table where they were sitting: beer for him, white wine for Scott, red wine for Russell.

'Thank God that's over,' he said, sitting down heavily.

'Yes,' agreed Scott.

'And just because the army refused him,' said Neville.

'Well, in his eyes the army refused him because they didn't think he could kill people,' explained Russell. 'He killed to show that he could. And he used a different way of killing each time to show how good he was.'

'Crazy,' said Neville. 'Completely mad.'

'Yes,' agreed Russell. 'But to him it was logical. He was just trying to show the army they'd made a mistake. Serial killers often think they're behaving logically.'

'But logically in a crazy way,' said Scott.

'Yes,' replied Russell.

'And this is what? Your third or fourth serial killer?' asked Neville.

'Third,' replied Russell. She drank a little of her wine. 'All three very different in some ways, but very similar in others.'

'How do you mean?' asked Scott.

'Well, the first,' began Russell, 'was a woman, a nurse actually, who killed some of the old people she visited at home. In her mind they were too old to look after themselves and so they shouldn't be allowed to live.'

Russell drank some more wine.

'The second,' she continued, 'was a man whose girlfriend left him about five years before. Since then he'd had great difficulty in his relationships with women. The problem built up and up, and eventually he started killing young women in their twenties with blonde hair. Girls who reminded him of his ex-girlfriend.'

'And now a guy who wants to show the army that he knows how to kill, so that they'll let him join up,' added Scott.

'Exactly,' replied Russell.

'And how are they similar?' asked Neville.

'They show just how little it can take to turn the balance of the human mind upside down,' answered Russell. 'A failed attempt to join the army, breaking up with a girlfriend, being in a job where you end up hating the people you're supposed to be helping – these are things that people often experience at some time in their lives—'

'But it doesn't usually turn them into killers,' interrupted Scott.

'No, it doesn't,' said Russell. 'Normal people manage. They move on. They get a different job; they get a new girlfriend. But for a very few people it changes the balance of their minds just enough. They develop a strange, kind of poisonous, murdering logic that drives them to kill. And, having killed once ...'

Russell stopped speaking and looked down into her glass.

Scott put her hand on Russell's arm.

'It's over now, Fiona,' she said.

Russell looked up.

'Yes, it is,' she agreed. 'Until the next time.'

After reading

读后活动

1. Choose one of the characters and write a few paragraphs about them describing what sort of person they are.
2. Write either a) DS Scott's police report of the case or b) Jonathan Greene's newspaper article about the case.
3. If you were making a film of this story, which famous actors would you choose to star in the main roles?
4. Think of another title for *Man Hunt* and explain why it would be good.
5. Write an email to the author, Richard MacAndrew, saying what you liked and didn't like about the story.
6. Make a quiz about the story for the other students, e.g. some True/False questions or some correct/incorrect sentences.
7. Write a monologue, like the ones which start each chapter, by Terry Reid, expressing his thoughts as he sits in jail in Richmond after being caught.
8. Why did Terry Reid fail in his goal of killing lots of people in different ways? Write around 150 words to explain your ideas.

Learning guide | 学习指导

Chapter 1

New words 生词

- amazing /əˈmeɪzɪŋ/ *a.* 令人吃惊的
- backpack /ˈbækpæk/ *n.* 背包
- binoculars /bɪˈnɒkjələz/ *n. pl.* 望远镜
- experience /ɪkˈspɪəriəns/ *n.* & *v.* 经历，体验
- hiking /ˈhaɪkɪŋ/ *n.* 徒步旅行
- intend /ɪnˈtend/ *v.* 打算
- largish /ˈlɑːdʒɪʃ/ *a.* 相当大的
- moorland /ˈmɔːlənd/ *n.* 荒野
- photographer /fəˈtɒgrəfə(r)/ *n.* 摄影师
- presumably /prɪˈzjuːməbli/ *ad.* 推测起来
- stretch /stretʃ/ *v.* 伸展
- stuff /stʌf/ *n.* 物品，东西
- unconscious /ʌnˈkɒnʃəs/ *a.* 失去知觉的
- vehicle /ˈviːəkl/ *n.* 交通工具
- wallet /ˈwɒlɪt/ *n.* 钱包

Phrases & expressions 短语和表达

- ace of spades 黑桃 A
- dress in ... 穿着……
- keep oneself to oneself 不与人来往
- make inquiries 进行调查

- pick up sth. 捡起某物
- scene-of-crime tape（犯罪现场）警戒带

Cultural notes 文化点滴

- Detective Inspector: 缩写为 DI，刑侦督察。Detective Sergeant，缩写为 DS，刑侦警长。英国的警衔由低到高主要有：constable（警员）、sergeant（警长）、inspector（督察）、superintendent（警司）、commissioner（警务处长）等。
- GPS: Global Positioning System 的缩写，全球定位系统。GPS 是一个高精度、全天候和全球性的无线电导航、定位和定时的多功能系统。GPS 技术已经发展成为多领域、多模式、多用途、多机型的国际性高新技术产业。
- pub: 酒馆，正式说法是“public house”。主要提供啤酒和威士忌。这些酒馆主要是为了提供一个让人放松、和朋友相聚闲聊的场所。

Reading exercise 阅读练习

Answer the following questions.

a) Different sections of the text in each chapter are printed in different ways. Why did the author do that?
b) Why did the murderer choose the particular place to kill the walker?
c) How did the murderer feel after he had killed the walker? Why?
d) Why did he kill this man?
e) Why do you think the killer put the playing card in the dead man's wallet? What does the policeman say about it later?

f) What do you find out about the dead man?

Chapter 2

New words 生词

- analyst /ˈænəlɪst/ *n.* 分析员
- available /əˈveɪləbl/ *a.* 可获得的
- avoid /əˈvɔɪd/ *v.* 避开
- badly /ˈbædli/ *ad.* 非常
- blonde /blɒnd/ *a.* 金发的
- divorced /dɪˈvɔːst/ *a.* 离异的
- embarrassed /ɪmˈbærəst/ *a.* 尴尬的
- exhausted /ɪgˈzɔːstɪd/ *a.* 筋疲力尽的
- interrupt/ˌɪntəˈrʌpt/ *v.* 打断
- investigation /ɪnˌvestɪˈgeɪʃn/ *n.* 调查
- medium /ˈmiːdiəm/ *a.* 中等的
- psychologist /saɪˈkɒlədʒɪst/ *n.* 心理学家
- stick /stɪk/ *v.* 刺，戳

Phrases & expressions 短语和表达

- carry out sth. 执行某事
- put into action 实施
- speak well of ... 称赞……
- turn off 转向，拐弯

Cultural note 文化点滴

- North Yorkshire: 北约克郡，英国英格兰北部的一个郡。建于 1974

年，首府诺斯阿勒尔顿。东临北海，北与克利夫兰都市区毗邻，西部为奔宁山地，东部是北约克高沼地（于 1952 年辟为国家公园），中部是约克郡谷地。北约克郡湿地是一片景色奇妙的荒野之地，有紫色的石楠花、山石嶙峋的海岸、古老的石头农舍和四处游荡的长毛绵羊。

Reading exercises 阅读练习

1. The killer did these things in the second killing.
   True or False?
   a) He drove his car to the place of the killing.
   b) He walked on the paths.
   c) He stopped to enjoy the beautiful views.
   d) He used a knife.
   e) He talked to his victim before killing her.
   f) He didn't leave a playing card on her body.
   g) He didn't enjoy this murder as much.
2. Which new character is introduced in the second part of the chapter? What is her job?
3. What is a serial killer?
4. What made the police and Russell think that these murders were done by a serial killer?
5. What information did Russell say was likely to be true about the killer?
6. What happened at the restaurant of the Half Moon Hotel?
7. How did Jonathan Greene anger DI Neville?
8. What do you think DS Scott wanted to say to Greene at the end of the chapter?

Chapter 3

New words 生词

- ambition /æmˈbɪʃn/ *n.* 野心，抱负
- crossly /ˈkrɒsli/ *ad.* 发怒地
- explode/ɪkˈspləʊd/ *v.* 爆炸；勃然大怒
- odd /ɒd/ *a.* 奇怪的
- oldish /ˈəʊdɪʃ/ *a.* 稍老的
- private /ˈpraɪvət/ *a.* 私人的
- raise /reɪz/ *v.* 提起，增加
- receipt /rɪˈsiːt/ *n.* 收据
- strangling /ˈstræŋglɪŋ/ *n.* 扼死，勒死

Phrases & expressions 短语和表达

- breaking news 重大新闻
- look into ... 观察……，调查……

Cultural note 文化点滴

- internet café: 也作 cybercafé，网咖，也就是网吧。提供互联网连接服务的公共场所，通常提供快餐和酒水。1994 年，世界上第一家网吧在英国伦敦开业。

Reading exercises 阅读练习

1. Match the beginnings and endings.

______ a) The killer sent the text message

______ b) The killer doesn't tell us

______ c) The killer wants some people to know

______ d) The killer says that some people

______ e) The killer says that he wants to

1) that he is successful at what he does.

2) strangle his third victim.

3) to the journalist.

4) prevented him from achieving his ambitions.

5) how he knows the journalist's phone number.

2. Why did the police keep Greene's phone?

3. Which of these things did Neville, Scott and Russell discuss?

a) The fact that both victims were at Avon University, Bristol.

b) The fact that both of the victims were walkers.

c) Whether the female victim's husband might be the killer.

d) Why they haven't found the killer's car or clothes.

e) Jonathan Greene's journalism.

4. What happened at the end of the chapter?

Chapter 4

New words 生词

- bluish /ˈbluːɪʃ/ *a.* 浅蓝色的
- disbelief /ˌdɪsbɪˈliːf/ *n.* 不相信
- overnight /ˌəʊvəˈnaɪt/ *ad.* 在夜里；一夜之间；突然
- yawn /jɔːn/ *v.* 打哈欠

Phrases & expressions 短语和表达

- dry-stone wall 干砌石墙
- in one's sixties 某人 60 多岁时
- stay up well into the night 熬到深夜
- straighten up 直起身

Cultural note 文化点滴

- CCTV：Closed Circuit Television 的缩写，闭路电视监控系统。系统通过摄像机及其辅助设备（镜头、云台等），直接观察被监视场所的情况，同时可以把监视场所的情况进行同步录像。

Reading exercises 阅读练习

1. Complete this summary of what the killer tells us.

He met his third victim when he was walking down the __________. They knew each other. The man invited the killer to have a __________ in his house. The victim had been a __________. The killer strangled him. He also broke the victim's __________. The killer wasn't sure what to do because he hadn't __________ this murder like the others. He decided to __________ the body to the countryside. He thought that the police wouldn't __________ the man's house if the body wasn't found there, and so he would be safe. He also decided to __________ a car to take the body away in.

2. Put the following events in the order in which they happen:

a) Scott talks to Jonathan Greene in the pub.

b) Russell tells Neville and Scott she thinks it is the act of killing which is important for the murderer.

c) The police visit the scene of the crime.

d) Greene says that he is investigating something to do with soldiers.

e) Russell, Neville and Scott have a meeting.

Chapter 5

New words 生词

- forensics /fəˈrensɪks/ *n.* 法医；取证技术
- freeze /friːz/ *v.* 使定格，锁定
- shot /ʃɒt/ *n.* 开枪，发射
- sticker /ˈstɪkə(r)/ *n.* 贴纸
- zoom /zuːm/ *v.* 变焦

Phrases & expressions 短语和表达

- get used to ... 习惯于……
- zoom in ... 放大……

Reading exercises 阅读练习

1. Answer these questions about the killer with short answers.

a) Does he live on his own?

b) Why was stealing a car easy for him?

c) Why did he need a blanket?

d) Why wouldn't there be many walkers out?

e) Why was it good that there was grass at the roadside?

f) Where did he leave the three of spades?

g) What did he do with his clothes and boots?

h) What will his next murder be like?

i) When will the murder be?

2. Who said these things and to whom?

a) 'The first car behind the tractor is the one to watch. I think our man is driving it.'

b) 'He's looking at the effects of active service on soldiers who have been out in the Middle East and the Gulf ...'

c) 'That means he must have used his own car to come out here for the first two murders.'

d) 'You've got the list of soldiers. Go over to Catterick. Talk to them.'

e) 'First check the CCTV to see if you've got him coming back into Richmond yesterday.'

f) 'Yes, well, I'd like forensics to examine it as soon as possible. We think it may have been used by the killer ...'

g) 'Another one, sir,' ... 'In fact, this time there are two.'

Chapter 6

New words 生词

- database /ˈdeɪtəbeɪs/ *n.* 数据库
- vet /vet/ *n.* 兽医

Phrases & expressions 短语和表达

- calm sb. down 使某人平静

- take chances 冒险

Reading exercises 阅读练习

1. The killer says: 'Why they didn't want me, I just don't understand.' Who do you think 'they' are, and why didn't they want him?
2. How did the killer get the people in the car to open the window?
3. What did he look for after the shooting? Was he successful?
4. Why did he say the police 'would never find the gun'?
5. What did Russell find out about 10 cars from the CCTV film?
6. How did she find the names and addresses of the cars' owners?
7. Why did the bullet casing give important information?
8. Two of the soldiers from Greene's list that Scott investigated live in Richmond. What did Russell do with that information?
9. Why did Russell say 'Got you' at the end of the chapter?

Chapter 7

New words 生词

- drowning /ˈdraʊnɪŋ/ *n.* 溺水
- major /meɪdʒə(r)/ *n.* 少校
- mathematical /ˌmæθəˈmætɪkl/ *a.* 精确的；严谨的

Phrases & expressions 短语和表达

- grandfather clock 落地式大摆钟
- like a well-oiled machine 像运转顺利的机器
- turn in on oneself 不与他人往来

Reading exercises 阅读练习

1. Put what the killer does in the correct order:
   a) He decides to make the next killing a drowning and do it the next day.
   b) He hides the gun in a box in a suitcase in the garage.
   c) He leaves the stolen car in the Gallowfields Business Park.
   d) He goes back home.
   e) He decides to put a sticker on the map already to mark the next day's murder.
   f) He goes for a walk because he doesn't want to talk to people at home.
2. What do these things refer to?
   a) red Ford Focus KV06EUU
   b) seven thirty in the morning
   c) a part-time gardener
   d) a Tariq nine-millimetre
   e) four years
   f) unnaturally tidy
   g) Barney Beck
3. Why didn't Terry get into the army?

Chapter 8

New words 生词

- anorak /ˈænərək/ *n.* 带风帽的厚夹克
- handcuffs /ˈhændkʌfs/ *n. pl.* 手铐
- physically /ˈfɪzɪkli/ *ad.* 身体上

Phrases & expressions 短语和表达

- close in on ... 包围……，围住……
- stepping stone 垫脚石

Reading exercises 阅读练习

1. Why did Terry Reid choose Barney Beck as his next murder place?
2. What does he tell us about his relationship with his parents?
3. What does he tell us about his brother, Alan?
4. How are the murders connected to the refusal by the army?
5. Are these things True or False?
   a) Russell went with Scott and Neville to Barney Beck.
   b) Neville made Russell stay in the car.
   c) When Scott looked over the wall Terry was drowning a woman.
   d) Terry Reid pointed a gun at Scott.
   e) Reid hit the woman on the head with a stone.
6. What did Reid pretend to have when he told Russell to get in the car?
7. What did Russell do to Reid?
8. What two other serial killers cases had Russell worked on?
9. What do you understand by Russell's final words?

Translation
参考译文

罪案追凶

第 1 章　殒命荒野

第5页

第一次杀人很顺利。事实上是完美，虽然我一直都知道会如我所愿。我做了周密计划，安排、组织——这些事我很擅长。现在我发现我也擅长杀人。

早上6点钟，我开车左拐驶离公路朝着谭山的方向而去。英格兰海拔最高的酒馆就在谭山。但是那儿只有那个酒馆，没有别的——没有房子，也没有其他建筑。最近的村庄在8公里开外，最近的商店在12公里开外。这里是寸木不长的荒郊野外。过一会儿当太阳升起来的时候，会有令人惊叹的景观，但是我对此不感兴趣。

我继续沿着土路穿过荒野之地，直到从公路上看不见车了才停下。这里并没有太多车辆。

我下车伸了个懒腰，享受着初秋刺骨的凉气。为了在这荒野晦暗的绿草衬托下不那么显眼，我穿着草绿色的徒步衣和靴子。我从车后座取出一个旧的棕色双肩背包，检查里面的物品。包里有一张地图、一瓶水、一副手套、一个望远镜和几块三明治。我取出手套戴上。我还有一台手持全球定位系统——我要去的地方没有路。在很多方面，我正走向未知之路。这是一次发现之旅，一次自我承诺已久的旅行。

第6页

我花了两个小时穿越野地走到了我想去的地方——两个小时好像就一会儿工夫。我的内心兴奋和紧张参半。我脑海里闪过各种可能即将发生的情况——但是我知道我会成功的。

最终我到达了我事先选好的地方。一座荒废已久的旧房子坐落在一条暗褐色的小溪旁，小溪沿山边哗哗地流淌着。这座房子没有屋顶，一面墙也塌了。四周有成堆的旧石块。我找到一块用右手掂着很舒适的石头，够重并且棱角锋利。等会儿我会用到它。

一条小路蜿蜒曲折地通向山坡，经过房子和小溪上的一座木桥。对于徒步的人来说这条小路很有名，尽管还没有特别广为人知。一个徒步者在这个明媚的秋日清晨走这条路的可能性很大，但不可能是一群人。稍后，当尸体被发现时，警察会认定杀手和步行者是从同一条小路来的，而不是从无路的荒野来的。他们会从错误的地点开始搜查。我的选择没错。

第7页

我脱下手套，从背包里拿出望远镜和一个三明治，坐在一块大石头上等待。从我所在的地方，我能看见任何从远处走来的人，但是他们很难看到我。

我刚好吃完三明治，一个男人就出现在远方，并朝我走来。我迅速戴上手套，捡起我选好的石头，然后藏身在房子的后墙后面等着。我的心跳开始加速，我深呼吸让它慢下来。我脑海中浮现出那个男人走近的画面。我变得兴奋起来，紧张感消失了。我听到走在土路上的脚步声，近了，更近了。我举起石头。这是关键时刻。

然后一切就结束了。

第8页

那人侧身倒在我脚边的地上，略长的花白头发散落在脸上。他闭着双眼，但眼皮底下还在动。我脱下左手手套，触摸他的颈侧。他没死，只是昏迷了。我看着他。就是这一刻——我想要经历的一刻，我承诺我自己的一刻。我又狠狠地击打了他，石头的边缘穿过骨头深深地刺进他的头部，然后他就一动不动了。

我俯视着这个男人，心里五味杂陈。我做到了！我感到兴奋、飘飘然、无可比拟，觉得自己技艺高超、强壮无比、不可战胜。我还活着。

我把石头抛得远远的，心里想着：让警察去找吧。他们从中什么也发现不了。

然后我从上衣口袋里掏出一张扑克牌，在死者的外套里找到钱包，把牌放了进去，再把钱包放回原处。

随后，我拾起我的双肩背包，返回到我的车那儿。

这只是开始。我能做给他们看，我能证明他们都错了，我能让他们看到我的真本事。

第9页

* * *

下午四点，刑侦督察查尔斯·内维尔从一辆深蓝色的警用路虎车里下来，车停在投降桥附近北约克郡寒冷的荒野之中。大约一个小时前，有人拨打紧急电话报告发现了一具尸体。20 分钟后第一批警察到达现场并确定不是自然死亡。内维尔立刻被召回。本来轮到他休息，他和妻子正在外面。他为家里购置厨房新设备一事突然间变得没那么重要了。

当内维尔从车里下来时，一个留着一头黑色短发的年轻女人向他走过来。那是刑侦警长海伦·斯科特。

“我是几分钟之前到这儿的，”斯科特说道，“尸体就在那边那栋建筑后面。”她挥着一只手指向一栋坍塌了一半的破旧无顶建筑。

内维尔能够看见黑黄相间的警戒带已经围住了那栋建筑和荒野的一大片区域，还有三辆路虎车和其他几辆越野车停在建筑物附近。

第10页

当内维尔跟着斯科特走向建筑物的时候，他抬头望向天空。厚厚的乌云开始从西边飘过来。

“约克郡的天气，”他指着天空，心情不好地说，“希望我们处理完这儿的工作之前不要下雨。”

内维尔来自东南部。尽管十年来他都住在约克郡，但还是没有适应这里的天气。太阳出来的时候，这里确实是一个特别的地方，但是在一天当中经历四季也是件稀松平常的事。

“是的。”斯科特附和道。

在那栋建筑的拐角处他们看到了凯·哈丁。她是一名法医，正俯身面对着一个穿着徒步衣和靴子的中年男子的尸体。这人还背着双肩背包。哈丁听到警探们过来就站了起来，立刻开始交谈。

“查尔斯、海伦，”她边说边用目光先后扫过他们俩，然后看向尸体。“现场我们发现的是一名 50 到 55 岁之间男子的尸体，推测他是出来散步。有人用力击打了他的头部侧面两次，有可能是用一块石头。”

“死亡时间呢？”内维尔问。

第11页

“今天上午 8 点到 10 点之间，我推测。”哈丁回答。

“还有别的吗？”内维尔问。

“暂时没有，”哈丁答道，“照相师一干完他的活儿，我就把尸体运走。我会把他的背包和从他口袋里找到的东西留给你们。”

“好，谢谢。”内维尔说。内维尔的心情好了点儿。哈丁是数一数二的——表达清晰、专业，从不说废话。他就欣赏她这一点。他再次望向天空，然后看了看手表。他们得快点儿了。他转向斯科特。

“我们会有充足的日光，”他说，“但天知道还有多久会下雨。把这个区域搜查一下——范围越大越好，越仔细越好。我们显然要找任何可能有用的东西，尤其要找到那块让他致命的石头。”

“好。”斯科特回答。

“谁发现的尸体？”内维尔问。

“当地一对夫妇，”斯科特答道，“他们在那边的那辆绿色路虎车里。”她指向那边。

“我过去跟他们聊聊，”内维尔说，“然后我们得考虑找一间办案室。里斯是最近的村子，也许那儿有。”

第12页

斯科特点点头。她和内维尔在最近的城镇里士满的警察局有办公室，但那儿离这里也有差不多 20 公里远。内维尔想要比那儿更接近现场的地儿。他们可以把一个移动办公室搬过来使用，或者他们可以在附近借用一个大房间。

“好，”她说道，“我就从这儿开始搜索。”

* * *

第二天早上 8 点，内维尔、斯科特和 15 名警察组成的团队在里斯纪念堂碰头，那里是他们新的办案室。这个很大的空房间一般是用作孩子集体游戏、开演唱会、乐队排练等。现在里面摆满了桌子、椅子、电脑、电话，还有一群警察。

内维尔面向他的团队站着，他的灰白头发和脸上的皱纹暴露了他的年龄。斯科特在他旁边。他们都没怎么睡。他们身后是一个白板，上面贴着一个男人的脸部照片。

“好，”内维尔开始说道，“首先，说一下我们知道的。这人是马修·肯沃西。”

他指着照片。

第13页

“他是昨天下午 3 点被本地一对出来遛狗的夫妇发现的。他的死亡时间大概是昨天上午 8 点到 10 点之间。有人用一块石头敲击他的头部侧面两次。我们已经找到了那块石头，但大家都不知道能否从石头上发现什么线索。”

第14页

他后退一步，看向斯科特。

“该你了。”他说。

“肯沃西是自己一个人来这里的，他来徒步旅行，”她开始说，“他住在里斯这里的马顿舒尔德酒店。他是几天前来的，之前没有来过这里。他很友好，但是不爱与人交往。”

她清了清喉咙继续说。

“昨天上午他从自己的车里出来，打算从投降桥开始绕个圈徒步 8 公里。我们在桥附近找到了他的车。”

斯科特随后指着她旁边桌上的一大堆塑料袋。

“我们已经彻底搜查了他房间里的物品，没有什么重要的东西。我们检查了他徒步时带在身边的东西。他只带了徒步者通常会带的东西——地图、全球定位系统、帽子、手套、三明治、水——但是有一样东西不同寻常。”

斯科特拿起一个塑料袋，举起来让每个人都能看见。袋子里面是一张扑克牌。

“黑桃 A，”她说，“在他的钱包里。他的房间里没有其他扑克牌。大家有什么想法吗？”

房间里所有的脑袋都在摇晃。

第15页

内维尔又向前走了一步。

“好，”他说道，“肯沃西是单身，住在布里斯托尔。那儿的警察正在查访。在这里我们也有活儿要干。我想让你们当中的 4 个人走一走肯沃西打算走的那 8 公里路。凶手可能跟在他后面，也有可能从相反的方向来。两人一组，分成两组——一组跟肯沃西同一个方向走，另一组从相反的方向走。沿途检查一下能否找到有用的东西。”

内维尔从桌上捡起一摞照片，把它们交给斯科特。

“我要你们其他人在里斯挨家挨户走访调查，”他说道，“这是个小地方，大家都相互认识。随身带上肯沃西的照片，看看有没有人认识他，或者跟他交谈过，或者看到过谁跟他交谈过。刑侦警长斯科特将会告诉你们具体的任务安排。”

内维尔转身刚想离开房间，一个声音从后面传来。

“长官。”

内维尔转过身。

“什么事？”他说。

一个警察举起一只手示意刚刚是他在讲话。

第16页

“怎么了？”内维尔问。

“黑桃A，长官，”这个警察说，“我刚想起来——它是死亡之牌。”

第2章　一个连环杀手？

第17页

我等了十天才决定再次杀人。我本来可以等得再久一点儿，但是我想要再次体验那一美妙感觉。我特别想要体验那种愉悦的感觉、成功的感觉、证明我完全正确的感觉。我已经看了报纸，警察对于发生的事情似乎没有头绪。我认为不会有被发现的危险。我是正确的。

我决定采用跟此前相同的基本方案。我会把我的车停在一个地方，然后在一个完全不同的地方找一个“不情愿的助手”。

但是，我对自己的计划做了一些改进。首先把我的车暴露在某地。徒步者会把他们的车随便停在北约克郡的乡下，没人注意他们的车。但是现在，也就是事发十天之后，一辆似乎是藏匿起来的车倒是可能引起警察的注意。

其次，我打算在傍晚实施我的计划。我希望这意味着直到第二天早晨尸体才会被发现，那样会给警察增加难度。

第18页

另外一个改变就是用匕首。我决定要体验不同的杀人方法。

最后，我将走小路到达我选定的地方。在约克郡的这个区域有许多小路，很难永远避开它们。当然，警察有可能把我的靴子或衣服和他们在小路上找到的东西匹配。但是我已经考虑到这些。这次以及未来的每次冒险之后，我都会把我穿戴的或携带的所有东西烧掉。我很聪明，不是吗？比警察更聪明，我认为。

我从格林顿出发开车驶向雷德迈尔，然后把我的车停在大概在两个村庄中间的荒野上。接着，我开始往回越过小山朝里斯的方向走去。虽然天空乌云密布，但一年当中的这个时候还是挺暖和的。

约克郡谷地的乡村非常美：山和谷连绵起伏，荒野遍布山顶，沉睡的村庄和农场坐落在谷底。对于约克郡人来说，约克郡是“上帝的土地”。但我不是去那儿欣赏自然美景的。

第19页

我花了好几个小时的时间才穿越完全空旷的荒野到达我在寻找的地方——一座小建筑。那里一般是空的，结队出来打鸟的人有时会用到它——但不是今天。小建筑刚好在这个地区的一条主路旁边，从这儿可以看到山谷上下的美景。

我从双肩背包里取出匕首和一张地图，坐在建筑后面等候。有可能今天这么晚了没人会从我身边走过。但是，只要有机会我就会做好准备。

在大约半个小时之后，我看到远处有一男一女，但是他们还没有靠近我就转身下山朝山底的小河走去了。我很幸运，因为杀两个人可能有点儿困难。我把一次杀俩的机会留在下次用枪的时候。

不久之后，我看到一个女人独自从对面过来了。很明显她刚好要经过我这里。这次我感到非常冷静，知道要做什么。时间似乎过得更慢了。当那个女人朝建筑走来时，我已经准备好了，并且开始期待我即将要做的事情。

第20页

她还在大概50米开外时我走了出来。我手里拿着地图，匕首也在同一只手里，但藏在了地图下面。当我走出来的时候，我看着地图，这样就不会吓到她。她一直朝我走来，这时我抬起眼看。她中等身高，金发，可能有30多岁。

我朝她微笑，看起来有点儿尴尬。

“我很抱歉，”我边说边微微摆动地图，但是确保匕首没露出来。“我好像有点儿迷路了。你可以指给我看现在我在哪儿吗？”

“当然。”她说完朝我站的地方走来。

她弯腰看向地图，我猛地向她左侧的胸口刺去。

空气似乎从她的身体里流出，发出了绵长而轻柔的声音。我直视着她的眼睛，感受这一刻，享受这一刻。她满脸震惊，努力想说什么，但是说不出。我放开匕首，她双膝跪地，然后侧身倒下。她闭上眼睛，死了。我静静站了一会儿俯视着她。我又成功了！我感觉太棒啦，如神一般。

第21页

我快速弯下腰把匕首从她的胸口拔出来，在她的外套上擦干净，然后把匕首放进我的背包。我从口袋里取出一张扑克牌，放进她的一个口袋里，这样警察就会知道是谁干的。

然后我步行两个小时返回到我的车那儿。在这快乐的两个小时里，我可以回味这一时刻。

* * *

菲奥娜·拉塞尔在她位于诺思阿勒尔顿的北约克郡警察局总部的办公室里。她刚刚看完最近一份关于网络犯罪的报告，靠着椅背坐着思考她得到了什么信息。尽管她为警方工作，但事实上她不是一名警察。她是一名犯罪分析师。那意味着，她是少数几个有可能看见与某一特殊犯罪有关的一切的人。她查看每一份文件、每一次讯问记录、每一份报告。她找寻模式、相似点、不同之处。在调查中她向上级警官汇报她的发现，然后就还要做些什么及哪些更多的信息可能有用提出建议。

正当她靠着靠背坐着的时候，手机响了。

“拉塞尔。”她立刻接起电话说道。

第22页

“我是北约克郡警察局的刑侦督察内维尔，”这个声音直奔主题，“我正在找一位有连环杀手破案经验的分析师。你的上司告诉我你就是我要找的人。”

拉塞尔感觉她后颈的汗毛都竖了起来。她此前参与过两起连环杀人案的调查，每一次结束的时候她都精疲力尽。每一次调查都是跟时间在赛跑，一场阻止杀手杀害更多人的赛跑。每一次调查都要求长时间耐心的工作，让她绞尽脑汁突破极限。每一次都以各自的方式给了她新的不同视角来看待痛苦；但是每一次也有它自身的兴奋点，带给她专业上的愉悦。

“我想是吧。”拉塞尔回答。

“好的，”内维尔说，“到目前为止，我们只发现两起谋杀，所以严格来说，这个人还不能被称为连环杀手。”

拉塞尔知道，一个杀手制造三起或更多谋杀才能叫作“连环杀手”。

“但是我不想等到第三起，”内维尔继续说道，“如果我们找不到他的话，我想毫无疑问将会有第三起甚至更多起。如果你了解我们目前的进展就会知道是为什么。我希望你尽早加入团队。”

第23页

拉塞尔注意到内维尔用了男性的“他”。曾经有女性连环杀手——但大部分是男性。

“好，”拉塞尔回答，“你们在哪里？”

“里斯，斯韦尔代尔。”内维尔回答。

拉塞尔看了看手表。“我大概一个小时之后到那儿。”她说道。

* * *

一个半小时后菲奥娜·拉塞尔坐在办案室后部的一张桌子旁。海伦·斯科特坐在对面的椅子上，把到目前为止的调查给她快速回顾了一遍。她已经在描述第二起谋杀案了。

“尸体是今天早晨在里斯郊外的山坡上被发现的，”她说道，“我一会儿在地图上指给你看。死者是一名32岁的女性，叫希拉·麦克法迪恩。她住在里士满，是一名护士。她在本地医院值夜班，经常在白天来这儿散步。她离婚了。她前夫住在本地，但是他们似乎相处得不错。他说她被杀害的时候他在家里，自己一个人。他不像是我们要找的人，但是不管怎样我们正在调查他——只是以防万一。她没有男朋友——至少没有那种大家都知道的男朋友。她有很多朋友，每一个人都对她赞誉有加。”

第24页

她伸出双手，好像要表明情况的绝望。

“似乎没有哪个人有杀她的理由。”斯科特补充说。

她停顿了一下。

“犯罪现场怎么样？”拉塞尔问道。

“和第一起谋杀一样，我们几乎一无所获，”斯科特继续说，“杀手直接一刀刺进麦克法迪恩的心脏。我们还没有找到那把刀。杀手把刀拔出来，在她的外套上擦干净，然后带走了。在现场我们找不到任何和凶手有关的线索。我们不知道他是怎么到达现场的，也不知道他是怎么离开的。事实上，我们并不知道凶手是男还是女。好像没有人看到什么奇怪的事情或人。”

斯科特伸手到邻近的桌子上拿起两个小塑料袋。每个袋里都有一张扑克牌——一张是黑桃 A，另一张是黑桃 2。

第25页

“再有就是这些。”她边说边把牌放在拉塞尔面前的桌子上。拉塞尔拿起其中一张看了看。

斯科特靠坐在椅子上看着拉塞尔。

“两张扑克牌，”斯科特说，“ A 是在第一具尸体上找到的，2 是在第二具尸体上找到的。你就知道为什么头儿认为我们现在是在对付一个连环杀手。当然，这些牌就是普通的牌，哪里都买得到。”

“是的。”拉塞尔说着，放下 A 又拿起 2。看着黑桃 2，她注意到在牌的中间有两个手写的字——“用刀”。她的后背感到一阵冰凉。

她放下扑克牌看着斯科特。她年近三十，留着黑色短发，穿着干练，明显是个聪明人。在这种调查中她会是一个得力的伙伴。每个人对任何可能性都要保持清醒和活力。她刚要说话，这时一个身穿西装的高个儿男人走向他们。他的脸上布满皱纹，黑发里夹杂着大量白发。

“刑侦督察内维尔，”他自我介绍道，“叫我查尔斯。你一定是菲奥娜·拉塞尔。”

第26页

他从桌子下拉出一把椅子坐下来。

“海伦已经告诉你我们的进展了吗？”他问。

“是的，她说了。”拉塞尔回答。

“然后呢？”内维尔问，“有什么新想法？”

在进一步了解调查情况之前拉塞尔不愿意讲太多。但是，作为团队里的新成员，她觉得需要告诉内维尔和斯科特一些事情。在阅读了大量关于连环杀手的案件资料之后，她可以总结出几点。

“我们可以做出一些理智的猜测，”拉塞尔说，“首先，我们最有可能正在找一名男性。大部分连环杀手是男性。曾经有过女性连环杀手，但有趣的是，她们通常更喜欢室内谋杀——在家里或可能在医院里——打个比方，一个护士杀死病人。”

拉塞尔看着斯科特和内维尔。

“而且我猜测他在25岁到40岁之间，”她继续说，“他需要足够成熟来计划和组织这一切。但是当超过40岁，人们一般就冷静下来，或者他们已经被抓住并关起来了。”

内维尔和斯科特面面相觑，然后看着拉塞尔。

“他好像确实很有条理，”拉塞尔补充道，“有条理而且聪明。所以你们在犯罪现场几乎一无所获。他也在行凶过程中成功避开了所有监控摄像机。我们是世界上被监控得最严密的国家，但是在谷地这里几乎没有监控——在城镇里没有太多交通监控摄像机，在建筑物四周几乎没有监控，而在乡下根本就没有。”

第27页

内维尔和斯科特边认真倾听边仔细观察。

“我还有理由相信我们正在寻找的是一个本地人——一个了解这个地区的人，”拉塞尔继续说，“我的意思是，我确信你们自己已经想到了这一点，两起谋杀都发生在杀手不太可能被打搅的地方。他显然非常了解这个地方。”

“没错。”斯科特说着把她的胳膊肘搁在桌子上。“但是为什么？为什么这些人被杀害了？”

“我不是心理学家，”拉塞尔说，“我只是研究事实。但是，看看这些扑克牌，我同意你们的看法，他会再次作案。我认为你们完全正确，这是一个连环杀手。”

她看着他们两个，微微一笑。

“当然，如果他继续杀人的话，我们就会捉住他。我们只需要幸运一次，他得一直走运才行。”

第28页

* * *

当天下午，附近的半月酒店的餐厅里都是记者，他们来自全国和本地的各类报纸、广播和电视媒体。查尔斯·内维尔面向房间站着，解释着最新进展——第二具尸体的发现及调查的进展。他不太喜欢跟记者打交道——事实上他不太喜欢记者——但是他知道他们偶尔也会协助调查。他已经做了一个简短的通报让他们高兴，但是对扑克牌的事守口如瓶。警察隐瞒一些信息是很正常的，这些没有通报的信息后来往往有用。

现在他正准备回答问题。两具尸体，还不知道杀手的信息，他料到时间不太好打发。他看到斯科特站在房间后面观察着。她冲他微笑，让他知道如果他需要，她就在那里。他点头致谢。

“因为时间关系我只能回答几个问题。”内维尔环顾房间说。有几个人询问了关于尸体发现地点的更多信息，还有人询问了关于男性死者和女性死者的一些问题。这时前排的一位女士说话了。

第29页

“我是吉马·泰勒，来自约克郡广播电台，”她说，“到目前为止发生了两起谋杀，你认为这是一个连环杀手干的吗？”

回答之前内维尔深吸一口气。

“正如你所知，这两人被杀害的方式完全不同，”他说道，“但是显然，我们对这个问题并无定论。”

靠近房间后面的一位男士举起一只手。

“我是乔纳森·格林，来自《伦敦晚邮报》。在每一个犯罪现场都发现了一张扑克牌，这是真的吗？那是不是意味着两起谋杀是一人所为？”

房间里刚才还算安静，但现在是一片死寂。这是新的信息。内维尔的脖子开始变红。斯科特看得出他在强忍怒火。内维尔引起了房间后面的斯科特的注意。她知道他想要干什么，于是向他点点头。

“我恐怕不能详细讨论在犯罪现场找到了什么或是没有找到什么。”内维尔说。

但是格林没有轻易放弃。

“在每个犯罪现场都发现了扑克牌，这确实能表明是同一个杀手所为吧？”格林问道，“甚至可能是一个连环杀手。”

第30页

突然所有的记者都开始交谈起来。有两个人离开了房间，从斯科特身边走过，边走边从他们的口袋里掏出电话。

“第二起案件调查还不足一天的时间，我们还不清楚在犯罪现场发现的哪些证据可能比较重要。”内维尔说道。他看看手表。“现在，女士们、先生们，恐怕只能到此为止了。”

他看着斯科特点点头，然后快速离开了房间。随着记者们站起来开始离开，现场闹哄哄的。当乔纳森·格林站起来的时候，斯科特注意到他很矮，相当胖，长着稀疏的浅棕色头发和一个大鼻子，相貌平平。当他走过斯科特身边的时候，斯科特转身走在他旁边。

“格林先生，”她说道，“我是刑侦警长斯科特。我想跟你聊聊。”

第 3 章　初期调查

第31页

给那个记者发送一条短信真是个好主意！当然，他不会知道是谁发的。我使用了一个特别的网站——aliamail.com。你可以用它发送邮件和短信，没人知道它们发自哪里。你开始使用这个网站的时候要提供一个姓名和邮箱地址，但是我用了一个假名字和一个网络邮箱服务。我还是从网吧发送的那条信息，不是用我自己的电脑。聪明吧，嗯？

很自然，警方会想要跟所有知道那个记者手机号码的人谈话。可能有成百上千号人。不管怎么样，警方都找不到我的名字。那个记者不清楚我知道他的号码。事实上，我怎么知道的？嗯，那是我的秘密。

所以，我很快就会得到我想要的。关于扑克牌的信息将出现在明天的报纸上，然后全国人民都会知道这些成果都是一个人的杰作。

全国人民都会看到我多么擅长我所做的事，看到我多么成功。最后，当我达到我的终极目标时，我会向他们证明他们错了。“他们”是谁？他们就是阻止我实现我人生中勃勃野心的人，他们错误并且残忍地夺走了我实现真正价值的机会。

第32页

然而我说得太多了，正如那句老话所说，“行胜于言。”我必须着手计划我的下一次冒险了。

首先我需要一些新衣服和靴子。我把上次穿的衣服烧掉了——我说过我会这么做——而每只靴子里面都放了一块大石头沉在了斯维尔河的河底。我不想买新衣服，二手的更好一些。附近有很多卖二手服装的商店。首先，二手服装更便宜——毕竟我只打算穿一次；再者，没人会认出那些是我的衣服。万一警方得到关于我的外貌的描述，那样也许能迷惑他们。

接下来我必须决定下次冒险的“方式”“时间”和“地点”。“方式”很简单。这次我想要接近一点儿，直接用手。一次扼杀，我用双手环绕住我的“助手”的咽喉。我想要体验这种使用双手所带来的身体亲密接触，而不是用一块石头或是一把匕首。我到现在为止总是旁观生命的逝去。这一次我要亲身感受生命的逝去。

第33页

关于“时间”，我想一定要快。我不能再等了。警方还找不到我，我不用担心他们。我对杀人引起的兴奋感越来越渴望，或者说是饥渴——对血液？老实说，我不在乎。对我来说这已经变成一种毒品——一种我需要的越来越多的毒品。

所以只有一件事还需决定——地点。我必须要研究我的地图。

约克郡谷地是一片辽阔的地域，但幸运的是，我非常了解这里。要找到合适的地方很简单。你可能想要知道在哪儿，但我不会告诉你。你很快就会知道，是一个适合私人聚会的安静地方。

* * *

“我跟你说——我不知道是谁发给我的。”乔纳森·格林搜遍了他的口袋，终于掏出一部手机。格林、内维尔和斯科特在里斯纪念堂后部的一个小房间里，内维尔决定把它用来做讯问的地方。那里有四把椅子和一张桌子；墙面是暗乳白色，上面有一些斯韦尔代尔的旅行观光照片，有一扇窗户正对着里斯汽车修理厂的后面。

第34页

格林把他的手机放在桌面上，然后将它推给内维尔。

“你自己看吧，”他相当愤怒地说，“没有发送者的号码。”

内维尔把手机推向斯科特。她拿起手机，打开后开始按按键。

“你认为来和我这个高级长官谈谈这件事不是个好主意吗？”内维尔的脸因为生气仍是红的，他的嗓音有些尖。

“拜托，督察。”格林回答道。他一只胳膊肘支在桌上，然后摊开手。“我是一名记者，收到一条关于谋杀案调查信息的短信——警察一定已经掌握的信息。我是去告诉警察他们已经知道的信息，还是提交这则报道，让《晚邮报》成为第一家发表这个爆炸性新闻的媒体？拜托，督察！现实点儿吧！”

“别告诉我要现实一点儿！”内维尔勃然大怒。他的拳头重重捶在桌上，脸色愈发阴沉。“这是一个谋杀调查。”内维尔一字一句地说，他的声音低沉，饱含怒火，他的视线锁定格林的眼睛。“你掌握的有可能，事实上很有可能，是直接来自杀手的短信。你不知道这对于调查来说有多么重要。它可能会让我们直接找到凶手，也许能帮助我们拯救一条生命，甚至多条生命。而你还没有意识到你应该做的第一件事就是让警方了解这件事？不，格林先生，你要现实一点儿了。向警方隐瞒信息是犯罪——这你是知道的。”

第35页

内维尔不再说话，但是继续盯着格林看。房间里一阵安静。最后，格林尴尬地移开视线，甚至被内维尔的怒气震撼到了。

斯科特抬头看了一眼，然后继续查看手机。

“他是对的，”她跟内维尔说，“那条信息没有发送者的号码。”

“得到你的号码很容易吗？”内维尔问，“有多少人知道？”

“不是太多。”格林回答道，由于问话变得更容易，他看起来开心了一点儿。“很可能只有我电话簿里的人。我没有向太多人透露我的电话号码，报纸也不会泄露出去。”

第36页

内维尔看着斯科特。

“那么我们会需要这部手机，”他说道，“务必给格林先生一张收据，然后安排人把他手机电话簿里的人都调查一下。”

“但是，嘿，你们不能这么做，”格林说，“我需要手机。”

“不行，”内维尔回转身对格林说道，“这是谋杀调查的一部分。现在出去吧。你很幸运不用在看守所过夜。还有，下一次——如果还有下一次——你务必要做正确的事。”

格林慢慢站起来，摇摇头，离开了房间。门关上的时候，内维尔看着斯科特。

“也调查一下他，”内维尔说，“而且你要亲自调查。我需要一个经验老道的人来做这件事。我想知道他当记者多久了，是否优秀，在《伦敦晚邮报》工作多久了。所有一切。我想知道为什么凶手选择给他发信息，是不是真是他干的。”

斯科特猛地抬起头。

“你不会认为他是……？”她开口说道。

“很可能不是，”内维尔回答，“但是小心谨慎没有坏处。”

* * *

第二天下午晚些时候，离第二起谋杀不足 48 小时，拉塞尔被叫到讯问室跟内维尔和斯科特谈话。从主厅传来阵阵嘈杂声。警官们正在打电话，问问题，核查信息，写报告。内维尔关上门，嘈杂声小了。

第37页

“好了，”他边说边抽出一把椅子重重地坐了下去。“菲奥娜，你到这儿已经 24 小时了，也了解了一切。你有什么可以跟我们说的？”

拉塞尔坐下来。斯科特抽出一个笔记本拿在手里。拉塞尔有一堆文件，都放在了桌上。

“呃，我不想让你们的期望值过高，”拉塞尔开始道，“但是有一条调查线索可能会有用。尽管‘可能’在这儿是一个重要的词。”

“继续。”内维尔说。

“布里斯托尔警方非常得力，”拉塞尔继续说，“他们已经搜查了肯沃西的房子，跟他的很多朋友和他的上级谈过。肯沃西在布里斯托尔的一所大学工作，是埃文大学医学院的讲师。”

第38页

“希拉·麦克法迪恩是一名护士。”斯科特说。

“确实，”拉塞尔回答，“但不止这些。事实上她是在埃文大学接受的护士培训。”

第39页

“所以她可能认识马修·肯沃西？”内维尔说。

“嗯，是吧。”拉塞尔不是很确定。

“但是……？”内维尔问。

“正如我说的，”拉塞尔继续说，“我不想让你们的期望值过高。希拉·麦克法迪恩在大学里的时间是12年……15年前。我还不知道那时肯沃西是否在那儿。他教医学，她学护理。好吧，科目是有点儿相似，但它们却是完全不同的课程，所以即使他们俩同时在那里，也可能彼此不认识。”

“我明白你说的‘可能’是重要的词的意思了，”内维尔说，“但是，这当然是一条值得跟进的线索。”

“对，”拉塞尔回答，“我已经给布里斯托尔警方写邮件，发了一份他们能够在那儿找到答案的问题清单。明天早上我要做的第一件事是提供另外一份问题清单供你的警官在这儿跟进。”

“好，”内维尔说，“还有其他的吗？”

“没有了，”拉塞尔答道，“正如我昨天说的，杀手是有条理的聪明人。到目前为止，他没有给我们留下什么线索。”

“那麦克法迪恩的前夫呢？”斯科特问，“有没有可能是他？他先杀了别人，然后是他的前妻，接着也许是第三个人——这样看起来就像是连环谋杀，但实际上他只想摆脱他的前妻。”

第40页

“一个令人讨厌的想法。”内维尔说。他的眼中闪过一丝微笑。“但确实值得考虑。你为什么不调查一下这种可能性呢？”

“好。”斯科特回答道，并记在了她的记事本上。

内维尔靠坐在椅子上。

“那么，”他仍然看着斯科特说道，“格林先生呢？告诉我们关于他你发现了什么。”

斯科特把记事本翻回几页。

“很显然乔纳森·格林是一位知名记者。他主要就职在南方的《伦敦晚邮报》，这就解释了为什么我从来没有听说过他。”斯科特的视线从记事本上抬起，“他通常报道犯罪事件，但是他也会在他认为人们违法的领域做独立调查。”

“比如说？”内维尔问。

“我已经拿到了他最近的一些报道的清单。”斯科特边答边翻到她记事本中的一页。“他报道的大部分内容只是直接的犯罪报告——发生了什么，谁做了什么，谁进了监狱，诸如此类的事。但是在去年年底，他写了一些大事件。其中一个是医疗保健服务领域的犯罪——清洁工偷了药品和设备并且全部拿到黑市上卖了。这篇报道使警方介入了调查。”

第41页

“我记起来了，”内维尔说，“我没有想到是格林。”

“另一则报道是采访杰里·安迪生。”斯科特继续说。

“他是谁？”拉塞尔问。

“20 世纪 80 年代伦敦有组织犯罪的大头目之一。”内维尔回答。

“他因为抢劫银行和谋杀被判了 15 年，刚从监狱释放出来，”斯科特继续说，“格林说服他接受了一个采访。他说了一堆的废话，如他是怎样看到了光明，放弃了他的犯罪生涯并且要改过自新。”

“注意，”内维尔补充道，“我听说他上次抢银行还有几百万没有找到，所以他完全有可能有实力改过自新。”

“不管怎么说，我猜那就是很难拿到格林的手机号码的原因，”斯科特解释说，“你不会想要安迪生半夜给你打电话的。即使是在最好的情况下，他也不是一个讨人喜欢的人。”

第42页

“当然。”内维尔回答。

斯科特又低头看她的记录。

“而最近他又在忙另一篇大报道，”她说道，“不幸的是它还没有见报，所以我也找不到相关的信息。他年初离开了几周去做些什么事情，但是……呃，我问的人也不知道，或者是不想告诉我。”

“我觉得你应该进一步调查，”拉塞尔建议，“弄清楚他出现在这儿的真正原因可能是值得的。我的意思是，一个记者从一家伦敦的晚报到这儿似乎很奇怪。”

“他也许是因为那条短信才来的。”斯科特说。

“我不这样认为。”拉塞尔回答道。她扫视了面前桌上的一些文件。“不，”她继续说，“他只是在查尔斯对记者说话之前几个小时才收到的信息。我记下了时间。”

第43页

“嗯，我同意菲奥娜的意见，”内维尔说，“你需要弄清楚更多关于格林的这篇报道的信息。”

正在这时敲门声响起。一位金色短发女士打开门朝房间里看。

“抱歉打扰了，先生，”她跟内维尔说，“又发现了一具尸体，是一位老人，在斯卡巴沃斯桥附近的哈克赛德路发现的。他的手里有张黑桃3。”

第 4 章　不一样的谋杀

第44页

今天我需要运气。对于这次谋杀我没有完全准备好。我看了我的地图，有了一些想法，但是没有最终决定去哪儿找我的“助手”。

这时他找到了我！

当然，我认识他。他住得离我很近。我以前在附近见过他，还跟他聊过天。下午在他家附近的街上，我经过他身边时跟他打了招呼。他邀请我进去喝杯茶，我接受了。

我们一踏进他的家，我就知道是他了。空气中有些东西好像不一样。他曾是一名警察，知道些事情。我对此很确定。我有一种不同寻常的感觉，部分是警告，部分是行动的召唤。

他转过身开始说话。我立刻知道我该干什么了。对于一个 60 岁出头的人来说，他身材保持得不错。但是我年轻、强壮、健康，而且我会出其不意。稍有迟疑只会让我眼睁睁地看着梦想破灭。我是不会让那样的事发生的。

第45页

我的双手向前卡住他的脖子，拇指用力压住他的咽喉，不让他呼吸。当他意识到我正在做什么的时候，他的眼睛圆睁着，充满了恐惧。

他回击，努力想把我的手扯离他的咽喉，但是我太强壮了。他击打我的手臂，但是他已经没有多少力气。他用手指甲抓我的眼睛，为了求生而做最后的无望的挣扎。

但是我正等着呢。我的头避开他的手向前撞去，我的前额正好击中他的鼻子，鼻骨断裂的恐怖声音响起。他的手无力地滑到身体两侧，他的脸开始呈现出一种青紫色。几滴鼻血沾湿了他的上嘴唇。他的舌头伸了出来。他的身体在我手上死沉死沉的，我轻轻让他滑下去，让他躺在地板上。

然后我在他身边坐下。我气喘吁吁，心跳快得好像刚刚跑了100米。我可以感觉到脸上的汗水和心中的恐惧。恐惧？或者那叫兴奋？

第46页

我做了几次深呼吸，然后开始感到平静了一些。我看着他，摸了摸他的脖子。他彻底死掉了。

但是我不能像我希望的那样享受这一时刻，我还要做一个决定。我或是把尸体留在这里，或是把它运到其他尸体被发现的乡下。

我环顾四周。只有一点儿血迹，全在他的上唇上面，很快就干了。没有明显的打斗痕迹，没有证据表明我到过这里。但是我是一个计划者，一个谨慎的计划者。我知道我计划得越周全，我就会越幸运。所以我决定把尸体送到乡下。当然，警察会发现尸体被移动过——我在电视上看过很多犯罪片，所以知道这一点。但是他们不会知道尸体是从哪儿转移过来的，这一点也许很重要。这个房间里也许有某个小东西——皮肤、头发、衣物——可能会让警察找到我。但是如果他们不搜查的话就不会。

这是一个好计划。我感到一阵愉悦的波浪拂过我全身。

我从后门出去开始往家走。我需要偷一辆车——我显然不能用我自己的车做这些。我还需要一条毯子来盖住车后面的尸体，还有黑桃3。

第47页

* * *

海伦·斯科特把警用路虎车停在路边的草地上，离斯卡巴沃斯桥有几百米的距离。路的左边是一面干砌石墙，墙的另一边是一片旷野，向下延伸至谷底的河流。路的右边是草地、荒野和一些缀着黄花的低矮灌木丛。绵羊在荒野上悠游，正如每年的这个时候它们都会做的事情一样。这是夜幕刚刚降临的时候，天还没有完全黑，正在下着小雨。

斯科特和内维尔从路虎车里出来，朝一群站在山坡上的人走去。凯·哈丁——那位法医，正跪着检查一具男性尸体。他趴在地上，头转向一边，望着山坡。

内维尔和斯科特到达的时候哈丁站了起来。

“我们的人。”她看着内维尔说。

内维尔的眼神中透着疑惑。

“布赖恩·巴宁厄姆，”哈丁说，“他曾是莱伯恩的一名督察。他去年60岁生日之后就不工作了，然后搬到了里士满。”

“老天啊！”内维尔难以置信地摇头，“我知道，他的欢送会我在场。我跟他很熟。”

第48页

哈丁弯下腰再次查看尸体。

“恐怕这死相不太好看，”她说，“他是被勒死的。大概在他死的时候还被击中了脸部。”

“是同一个……”斯科特问道。

“是的。”哈丁回答，她直起腰把一个塑料袋递给内维尔。袋子里面是一张扑克牌——黑桃3。扑克牌中间写着“用手”。内维尔把它递给斯科特，斯科特看了一眼后又还给了哈丁。

“但是有不同之处，”哈丁边说边再次弯腰看了一眼，“尸体被移动过。”

“在这儿被杀然后移动的？”斯科特问，“还是在别处被杀然后移到这儿来的？”

“哦，在别处被杀然后移到这儿来的，”哈丁回答说，“我的意思是，现在他是趴着的。但是他死后我确定他短暂地仰面躺过，然后侧身躺了更久一点儿。”

内维尔看了一下四周的荒野，然后低头看向路边。

“拿一些警戒带，”他转向斯科特说，“尸体周围20米的范围内，一直到路边。搜查完毕前不准其他人踏入。”

第49页

“好。”斯科特边回答边点头向组里的几个警员示意，让他们按内维尔的命令行事。

“我的意思是‘搜索’，”内维尔继续说，“要仔细。我想要你们手脚并用。杀手肯定是开车来的，所以也在路边找找轮胎印子。”

“好。”斯科特回答。

“谁发现的尸体？”内维尔问。

“当地一个农民，”哈丁回答，“左边第一家农场，那个方向。”她指向右边的路。“他还得回来——说说关于他的羊的事。”

“好的，”内维尔说，“我们要跟他谈谈。”

“死亡时间？”斯科特问道。

“今天下午，”哈丁回答，“也许3点或4点。下雨前是一个相当暖和的下午，所以很难精确判断时间。”

“好，谢谢，凯，”内维尔说，“他交给你了。”

“他离婚了，”内维尔看着斯科特说道，“但是我认为应该有人通知他的前妻。我会去做这件事，我知道她住的地方。你在这儿处理一切，并且找发现尸体的农民谈一谈。大概一个小时之后我们在里斯碰面。”

＊　＊　＊

第二天早上 7 点钟，菲奥娜·拉塞尔在办案室收邮件的时候打了个哈欠。她睡了 3 个小时，熬夜阅读了布里斯托尔警方、里士满警方和里斯警方的报告。布里斯托尔警方连夜发来一封新邮件，但是里面没有任何有用的信息。她此时已经看了所有与前两起谋杀相关的资料，也看了到目前为止得到的第三起案件的信息。唯一让她感到怪异的是第三具尸体被移动过。为什么？他必须移动尸体吗？如果是，那为什么呢？

第50页

她正思索这些问题的时候，门开了，内维尔和斯科特手里端着咖啡走进房间。内维尔在说着话。

“……他们快要发疯了，”他说，“48 小时内发生两起谋杀案。”他看着拉塞尔。“记者们！”他带着情绪解释道，“就好像我们除了应付他们没有其他事情可做！我们可有的是事情要做。”

内维尔走进讯问室，把他的咖啡放在桌子上。

“杀手犯了一个错误，”他转移了话题说，“我对这一点确信不疑。他犯了一个错误，我们要充分利用这一点。”他看着拉塞尔。

第51页

“你怎么想的，菲奥娜？”内维尔问道，“我说的是，移动尸体。”

拉塞尔加入他们，一起都坐了下来。

“这很奇怪。”她回答。她想了一会儿，然后看着内维尔。

“到目前为止我们还没有看到任何监控录像，是吗？”她问道。

“在发现尸体的地方没有监控，”内维尔回答，“我们不知道要找什么，或者到哪里找。”

“现在我们也许知道了。”拉塞尔说。

“你是什么意思？”内维尔问道。

“嗯，我们现在知道巴宁厄姆是在 3 点稍后一点儿被杀害的。他的尸体是在大概 6 点 30 分被发现的。”她把一根手指放在嘴唇上，继续仔细思考。“我们的杀手可能住在斯韦尔代尔、阿肯格斯代尔，甚至温斯利代尔的一个村庄，但同样有可能住在附近的一个城镇。”

“有监控录像的地方。”斯科特说。

“聪明的想法。”内维尔说。他看着斯科特。“赶快，海伦。我们需要所有从里士满和莱伯恩到这儿的沿途监控录像。”

第52页

“还有卡特瑞克？”斯科特问道。

“是的，”内维尔回答，“也许还有巴纳德城堡。还有，让人把这些记者打发走。如果有时间的话我今天下午晚些时候会跟他们说的。”

斯科特起身离开房间。

“有任何来自布里斯托尔的消息吗？”内维尔转过身问拉塞尔。

“肯沃西和麦克法迪恩还是有可能互相认识，”拉塞尔回答，“现在我们知道他们同时在那所大学待过。但是，布里斯托尔警方还不能确定他们是否真的碰过面。”

“好，”内维尔说，“继续跟进他们的线索。那么麦克法迪恩的丈夫呢？有什么关于他的消息？”

“他是清白的，”拉塞尔说，“海伦派出一些警员去问了他的邻居，其中一个看到他在谋杀发生的时间里出门丢垃圾。”

“好，”内维尔说，“我想从我们的嫌疑人名单上划掉一个人也是一种进展。”

斯科特返回房间的时候，拉塞尔一脸疲惫地朝内维尔笑了笑。

“最新的这起谋杀确实存在一些疑点，”拉塞尔说，“首先是，为什么这次他移动了尸体？而且，巴宁厄姆以前是警察的这件事——重要吗？”

第53页

内维尔和斯科特都摇了摇头。

“不知道。”斯科特回答。

“其次是，”拉塞尔继续说，“他为什么要这样做？必须要有个理由，即使只是对他来说有意义。看看他的杀人方式：用石头敲击头部，用刀刺杀，勒颈。第一张牌上什么字都没有，但是第二张和第三张上写着‘用刀’和‘用手’。”

“就好像他在尝试用不同的方法来杀人。”斯科特说。

“确实如此。”拉塞尔回答。

一阵沉默。

“也许在显示他能做到。”斯科特提议。

更长的沉默。

“他似乎并不是从折磨受害人当中获得什么乐趣，”拉塞尔说，“我的意思是，一些连环杀手会花上一段时间——他们几乎都会玩弄他们要杀的人。”

“所以你觉得是杀人行为本身对他来说很重要，是吗？”内维尔问道。

第54页

“是的，我是这么想的。”拉塞尔回答。

* * *

那天上午晚些时候，斯科特没有买到奶酪三明治后，正从银街的面包店往回走，这时她看到乔纳森·格林走进了羊肩酒馆。他肩上背着一个大包，穿着一件有图案的灰色衬衫和一条灰色裤子。鉴于他的长相和体型，那打扮不怎么时尚。他看起来有点儿像一头小象。

“嗯，总会有办法知道他正在这儿做什么。”斯科特自言自语道。她等了几分钟，然后跟着他进了酒馆。

格林坐在炭火边的角落里，面前有一杯啤酒，他正在读《达林顿和斯托克顿时报》。当斯科特走向他的桌子时他抬起头来。

“看点儿轻松的东西，”他微笑着说，“我喜欢本地报纸。”从他说话的方式斯科特意识到他另有所指。

“对你来说，《达林顿和斯托克顿时报》还不够好？”斯科特问道，“和全国性的报纸还有伦敦那些日报不是一个级别的吧？”

“嘿，我是开玩笑的。”格林回答，他看起来有点儿被打击到了。

第55页

“是的，没错。”斯科特说，她暂时不会相信他说的话。

斯科特拉出一把椅子坐下。

“我想问你几个问题。”她说道。

格林什么都没有说。斯科特直视他的眼睛。

“如果你能此时此地回答的话会更好，”她说，“不要让我把你带到办案室去跟刑侦督察内维尔谈话。我想你也更喜欢这样。在督察看来，记者是人类最低等的职业。你也许已经注意到了。”

格林笑了。

“问吧，”他说，“我不能保证全部都能回答，但是我不介意跟一位迷人的女士交谈。”

一想到被格林搭讪，斯科特就感到有点儿不舒服，但她还是继续说了下去。

“正如你知道的，我们正在调查谁可能会有你的手机号码，特别是在北约克郡这里，”她开始说，“所以知道你在此地的原因对我们会有用。”

“啊！”格林叹了一声。

“我们知道你不是来这里报道谋杀案的。”斯科特说。

第56页

“啊！”格林又叹了一声。他咬着他的下唇，笑着说：“你有多想知道呢？”

斯科特不确定这是一个真正的问题还是一场搭讪，那对她来说并不那么重要。

“你是有多想见内维尔刑侦督察？”她看着格林反问道。她的眼神透着冷漠。

格林用手拂过他仅剩的头发。

“这真的很难……”他开口道，“我的意思是，我不会告诉任何人我的报道的事，直到——”

“今年早些时候你去哪里了？”斯科特打断他，“我知道你出国了一段时间。你去了哪里？”

格林停顿了一下，之后似乎是接受了他不得不回答的事实。

“中东。”他说。

“海湾？”斯科特问。

“没错。”

斯科特突然想到，是军队。卡特瑞克守备部队离里斯大概有 20 公里。在那里有超过 12 000 名士兵，他们全都参加过实战。

“军队。”她说道。

第57页

“是的。”格林说。

“你跟军人交谈了。”她说。这算不上一个问题。

“是的。”格林说道。

“在你手机的电话簿里我们没有找到任何军人的号码。”斯科特说。

“我告诉过你，我在电话簿里不会存很多号码。”他回答。

“但是你把号码给了一些军人。”斯科特说。

“是的。”格林回答。

斯科特拿出一个记事本，然后顺着桌面推了过去。

“我想要每一个有你电话号码的军人的名字。”她说。

“但是——”

“现在。”斯科特说。

格林伸出手。

“我可以告诉你一些人名，”他说，“但是不全。我在酒馆遇到的军人太多了。我们只是聊天。我没有问他们的名字，通常他们也不想让我知道。鉴于我调查的这类报道，如果他们的名字见诸报端，就会给他们的军旅生涯带来麻烦。他们必须要非常小心。”

第58页

斯科特拿出一支笔递给格林。她看着他的眼睛，什么也没说。

格林拉过记事本开始写起来。

“写完以后，”斯科特说，“你就可以告诉我你究竟在调查什么了。”

第5章　监控录像中的发现

第59页

我侥幸成功——但是我筋疲力尽！累得我从今天早晨一直睡到了中午。疲劳一部分是因为身体上的——首先是那场打斗，然后是搬运尸体；另一部分是因为心理上的——因为我还没有完全准备好这次冒险。我必须迅速思考，还要非常小心。

我起床时没有其他人在家。我煮了杯咖啡，然后思绪被拉回了昨天下午。我需要确定我没有犯错。

我走回家拿毯子，换衣服，取黑桃3。尽管我很着急，但是我步行——跑步会引起别人对我的注意。我把毯子、扑克牌和一副望远镜放进一个包里，然后出去找车。如果你知道怎样偷车，那就是一件容易的事——而我知道怎么偷车。

我把车开回我的“助手”的房子，停在房后，把尸体弄到后座，并用毯子盖上，然后我往里斯方向出发。一路上我在想把尸体扔在哪里：小路，安静的地方，我可以搬出尸体又不被人看到的地方。已经是下午4点左右，但是一下午都细雨纷纷。外面不会有太多的行人。我选定了一个极好的地方。

第60页

我沿着斯维尔代尔的道路开车，左转穿过斯卡巴沃斯桥，然后又左转开回格林顿和里斯。这里有荒野，上面的灌木丛可以遮掩尸体一阵子。我把车停在路边——路边有草，所以我不会留下轮胎印。然后我下车，用望远镜仔细查看了周围的乡野，没有人。

我开始快速干活儿，把尸体从后座搬出来。我抓住脚踝，把它拖上山坡，藏在一些灌木丛的后面。我把那张扑克牌放在那人的手里，环顾四周确保警察找不到什么，然后返回到停车的地方。

还剩下几件事情要做——扔了这辆车，换衣服，把我现在穿的衣物烧掉，把我的鞋子丢进河里。简单！

这一切发生得很匆忙，我对此很遗憾。但是既然已经结束了，我就能放松一下，回味并享受这一刻了。我可以把第三个标签贴在我的谋杀地图上，以显示第三具尸体将会被发现的地方——如果它还没被发现的话。

第61页

我还可以开始计划我的下一次冒险。我正品尝个中滋味，不单是人们可以看到我有多么强大和我能做到什么，我还能享受这种感觉。是每次杀人所带来的兴奋感，做出正确事情的肯定感。

下次会是两个人，双重快感。我将用枪。我已经到野外开过几枪来适应。枪里只剩5发子弹，我不知道我是否可以得到更多的子弹。所以，我想要离得近些，这样就不会失手。我也知道这次会发生在何时何地，应该是在夜幕刚刚降临，在路边。所以我需要再偷一辆车——但那不是问题。也许今晚有点儿早，也可能不早。我已经能够感觉到兴奋感在汇聚，我已经知道那种感觉有多么美妙。

是的，今晚。

* * *

那天晚上菲奥娜·拉塞尔在她的桌旁，正想着自己什么时候才能再次好好睡一觉。她伸手去拿咖啡，这时听到她的电脑上又收到一封邮件：报告前一天下午在里士满有两辆车被偷。两辆车被盗在里士满可算不同寻常。这个城镇不大，车不会经常遭到偷盗，同一天有两辆车被偷很奇怪。

第62页

一辆深绿色的迷你车深夜在集市广场被盗，一辆银色的斯柯达在下午 3 点 15 分到 3 点 45 分之间在盖洛菲尔兹商业园丢失了。斯柯达轿车被偷的时间大概在第三起谋杀的时候。所以，也许是一辆斯柯达。

拉塞尔把车牌号记录下来。然后她在电脑上打开一些监控电视录像，录像来自里士满的一台监控，能拍摄到通向斯维尔代尔和里斯的道路的情况。她按了“快进”键，直到右下角的时间显示是15:13:27。这可能是正确的时间，但这是正确的路吗？当然，偷车贼可能根本就不是杀手。他或者她，甚至可能都没有朝斯维尔代尔方向去。

拉塞尔按下“播放”键。车辆驶过，接着没有车驶过，然后有一辆车，接着很长时间都没有车。这条路车流量不大。她按了“快进”键，当更多车辆经过时，她又按了“播放”键。

时间显示 16:00:00。一辆红色小巴经过——这辆巴士从里士满到里斯，然后继续驶向斯维尔代尔——之后出现一辆农用车，后面跟着一串小轿车，然后就没有车了。

第63页

拉塞尔停下了录像回看。在农用车后面的那些小轿车挨得太近了。她定格了画面以便看个仔细。这串车最后面是辆宝马，然后是一辆奥迪、一辆福特、一辆路虎，但是第一辆是什么车？很难看清。

监控录像是黑白色的，所以看不清楚。

第64页

她放大图像并往图像下方移动，试图看清那辆车尾部的号码牌。号码牌被挡住了——路虎靠得太近了。她往回倒了几分钟，再次播放录像。这次她用了慢放。

当车进入画面，她定住了录像，把第一辆车的尾部放大。是的！是辆斯柯达——太好了。她又让录像慢慢开始播放。停！她可以看到车牌的一半，只有最后三个字母。它们和被偷的斯柯达的最后几个字母吻合。是的！太棒了！

就像有一股电流通遍她的全身，她的头脑感到轻松了。这种感觉几乎让她惊喜不已。

正在这时，斯科特走进房间。她的脸上带着兴奋的表情，但是当她看到拉塞尔时收回了表情。

“菲奥娜，你还好吗？”她担心地看着另一个女人问道。

第65页

拉塞尔挥挥手，回以满面笑容。

“我很好，我很好，”她说，“来看看这个。”

她把录像倒回到车流刚刚进入画面的地方。

“看这个，”她说，“看拖拉机后面的第一辆车。我想我们要找的人当时就开着它。”

她们认真观察录像，直到车在视线里消失。车正驶向远离监控的方向，所以不可能看到司机。拉塞尔把录像拉回到开始的位置，她们又慢慢看了一遍。然后拉塞尔停止了录像播放，看着斯科特。

“为什么你认为是他？”斯科特问道。

“车是在谋杀发生期间被偷的。”拉塞尔回答。

“啊，”斯科特说，“你认为他偷了一辆车而不是用自己的车——如果他有车的话。”

“是的。”拉塞尔回答。她伸手抓住斯科特的胳膊。“如果是他，他偷了那辆车，”她说，“然后从里士满开出来——也许他住在那儿。”她冲斯科特微笑。“他开始犯错了。”

拉塞尔放开斯科特的胳膊，站了起来。

第66页

“不管怎么样，”她说，“你来这儿是有重要的事情吧。”

“哦，是的。”斯科特说道，兴奋的表情又回到她的脸上。“我们去找查尔斯。我们需要交换意见。”

* * *

半个小时之后，内维尔、斯科特和拉塞尔围坐在讯问室里的桌子旁。

“我直接说吧，”内维尔看着斯科特说，“乔纳森·格林目前正在从事跟军方有关的调查。”

“是的，”斯科特回答，“他正在调查战时服役对那些曾经在中东和海湾地区服役过的军人的影响——主要是思想层面的影响，以及政府正在做些什么来帮助受到严重影响的军人。”

“我还以为他是一个犯罪调查记者。”拉塞尔说。

“他是，”斯科特回答道，“他认为政府做得还不够。很明显，他觉得他们的立场可以被视为犯罪。格林的哥哥曾经是一名军人，他受到严重影响以至于不得不离开军队。现在他从不出门。对格林来说，这是很私人的事情。”

“我明白了，”内维尔说，“你认为是一名军人给格林发送了关于扑克牌的信息——一名格林给过电话的军人。”

第67页

“那似乎确实很合乎逻辑，”拉塞尔说，“我的意思是，我们认为杀手就住在本地，是杀手发送的短信。杀手有格林的手机号码。他在这里唯一给过手机号码的人只有军人和少数记者。”

“格林把他的电话号码给了多少军人？”内维尔问斯科特。

“这就是问题所在，”斯科特回答，“他不知道。我已经拿到了六个人的名字，但他跟更多的人交谈过。军人们非常乐意跟他聊天。但是由于他的调查不太可能受到军队的欢迎，他们不太愿意把自己的名字告诉他。”

内维尔看着拉塞尔。

“你认为你在监控录像里看到了坐在被偷的斯柯达里的凶手，他在上起谋杀之后立刻就离开了里士满？”

“是的，”拉塞尔回答，“等下我要看看他是否是沿原路返回的，因为他会面向监控摄像头，我甚至可能会看到他。但是你知道监控画面清晰度怎么样。我不指望能告诉你他长什么样。”

第68页

她张嘴想说些别的，但是又停下想了想。

“怎么？”内维尔问。

“就我所知，”拉塞尔慢慢说道，仍在思索，“在前两起谋杀案发生的时候没有车辆被盗。我会核查这件事，但是我确信我是对的。”

内维尔和斯科特什么都没说，他们在等待拉塞尔说完她的观点。

“那就意味着在前面两起谋杀中他一定是开他自己的车来这儿

的。”拉塞尔说。

“所以很有可能那几天他都是开自己的车出现在监控录像里，”斯科特说，“如果他们还有录像的话。”

“目前他们不使用录像带了，”拉塞尔说，“都存在电脑里——硬盘上。录像可以保存更长时间，所以我们应该可以拿到。”

“好，”内维尔决定道，“菲奥娜，首先查查监控录像，看看是否可以找到他昨天晚上回到里士满的图像，然后查看前两起谋杀案发生时同一台摄像机拍下的录像。”

他转向斯科特。

“海伦，”他说，“你跟进军队这条线索。你有军人的名单了，到卡特瑞克去仔细盘查。跟他们聊聊，问些问题，找找看跟格林聊过天的还有谁。带几个警官一起去，这可能很重要。”

第69页

内维尔用手捋了捋头发，站了起来。

“明天能有一些新的进展告知记者还挺好的，”他说，“我不得不说我讨厌在全国性报纸的头版看到自己的照片。”

* * *

正当内维尔、斯科特和拉塞尔走回办案室时，他们听到一个女警官在打电话。

“好的，”她说，“是的，我也觉得很奇怪。嗯，我会告诉我的上司和……”这时她环顾四周，看到内维尔就在身后。“等等。我的上司就在这儿。你跟他讲吧。”

内维尔抬起眉毛。

“我是里士满的阿特金斯督察。是关于一辆被盗的车。”警官说。

内维尔接过电话。

“刑侦督察内维尔。”他说。他举起一只手示意斯科特和拉塞尔等一等。他们听到他结束了谈话。

第70页

“对……是的，我知道。我们刚刚在谈论这件事……是的，很奇怪……是的，嗯，我希望司法鉴定科尽快检查。我们认为凶手可能使用过这辆车……好，我把号码留给你……让他们一找到东西就尽快给我打电话。”

内维尔把电话还给警官，然后看着斯科特和拉塞尔。

“他们发现车停在和被偷的时候几乎同一个位置，”他告诉她们，“阿特金斯正让司法鉴定科检查。”

“在同一个地方很奇怪。”斯科特说。

拉塞尔陷入沉思中。“我在想为什么？”她问。

“你是什么意思？”内维尔问。

“为什么他把车开回原地？”她问，“一定有个理由。可能是离他住的地方较近——所以很容易到达，或者离他住的地方很远从而迷惑我们。”

斯科特走到门口又折回来，思考着。其他人看着她。

“时机，”她说，“时机很重要。我们知道死亡的时间：3点刚过的时候。4点的时候我们在监控里看到他从里士满开车出来。”

第71页

“确实。”拉塞尔回答。

“他一定是从犯罪现场附近偷的车。”斯科特说。

“车停在盖洛菲尔德商业园。”拉塞尔说。

“离巴宁厄姆的家不远。”斯科特补充道。

“那里可能是犯罪现场，”内维尔说，“尽管我们还没有在那里找到什么痕迹。”

这个时候办案室另一边的电话响了。

一个警官接了电话，然后看着内维尔。

“又一起，长官，”他说道，“事实上，这次是两个人。”

整个房间都安静了。拉塞尔瞪大眼睛。内维尔走过房间去接电话。在简短交谈之后，他放下电话转身看着房间。

“黑桃 4 和 5，用枪。”他说，“他在投降桥旁开枪打死了一对年轻情侣。”

他看着斯科特。

“我们走吧。”他说。

“长官？”拉塞尔问。她知道他们通常会叫名字，但是她想问些特殊的事情，更礼貌一点儿是上策。

第72页

内维尔看着她。她看得出来他知道问题是什么，也看得出来答案会是什么。

“你说。”他回答。

“我知道犯罪现场不是我通常该去的地方……”她开始说。

“可以，可以，快点儿，”内维尔回答，“拿上你的外套跟我们走。但是不要呕吐。”

“以前我见过尸体。”拉塞尔说。

第 6 章　接近目标

第73页

生命变得越来越好，还是死亡变得越来越好？不管怎么说，这又是一次完美的杀人。我很擅长于此。为什么他们不要我，我真是不明白。

我走到老火车站去给自己找辆车。老火车站现在是一家电影院，在它前面有一个停车场。如果车主正在看电影的话，我甚至可能在电影结束之前把车还回来。他或她甚至都不知道车被偷过。这完全取决于晚上的进展。

夜幕刚刚降临，天还没有完全黑。你也许认为我是在碰运气，在光天化日之下偷车。但是我动作迅速。我轻而易举地打开车门上了车，把枪放在乘客座位前的地上，然后发动了车，驶向里斯和斯维尔代尔。我知道我正在找什么——在谷地很多地方的路边有小型停车场。我会开车找到一个里面停着一辆车的停车场：也许有一对老年夫妇会停下来看风景，或者一对年轻情侣正在接吻和拥抱。对我来说都一样，我只是想证明我可以做到。

第74页

我先到了里斯。里斯纪念堂的灯亮着。我在报纸上看到警察拿它当办案室。开车经过这个他们因为想要抓住我而设立的地方似乎很滑稽。“你们有本事就来抓我，”我想，“但是你们不能，你们抓不到我。”

没有人把车停在里斯和莱斯韦特之间，所以我左转沿着去投降桥的路向斯维尔代尔开去。

沿路有一个浅滩，有条小溪漫过了路面，你不得不从水中开过去。这个浅滩很有名，因为它的画面总是在一个关于兽医的热门电视连续剧的开头出现。我小时候就看过那些节目，但是最近我只看犯罪节目。

我继续往投降桥方向开。当我开上山顶，俯瞰桥的时候，我可以看到，就在另一边停着一辆蓝色的车，车里面有人。是两个人，正是我要找的。

我从桥上开过去然后停下——但是没有离那辆车太近。我不想打草惊蛇。我偷车的时候就注意到在车后座有张地图。我想我又得用地图那一招了。

第75页

我把枪放进我的口袋，展开了地图，然后下车走了过去。

车里是一对年轻人。男的大概20岁，黑发，帅气；女的同龄，金发，很漂亮。他们刚才一直在接吻，但我一停车他们就突然停止了。

看到我走向他们，手里拿着地图，年轻女人打开了驾驶座的窗户。

“有什么能帮你吗?”她冲我微笑。

那时候我离她只有几米的距离。我也冲她笑了，拿出我的枪朝她的头部射去。她向前倒在方向盘上。

她的男朋友大叫着什么，但是他没有时间做任何事了。我把枪往左边挪了几厘米，也射中了他的头部。

我确认他们都死了，然后让两具尸体在他们的座位上坐直，这样他们看起来就像是还活着。最后，我探进车里，把黑桃4和5扔在后座上。

当你像这样开枪，子弹从枪的前端射出，托住子弹头的弹壳会从侧边被抛出，有时候抛出几米远的距离。有一个弹壳很容易就找到了，我捡起来放进了口袋。另一个不知道到哪里去了。我在草地和小灌木丛里搜寻了一番，但就是找不到。

第76页

几分钟之后我听到远处有车的声音。该走了。即使警察找到弹壳，也没什么关系。带走弹壳只是因为我谨慎，做事滴水不漏。警察真正想要的是枪。找到了枪和子弹他们才可能把它们匹配上。但是他们永远也找不到枪。

我回到车上就开走了。

尸体还要一段时间才能被发现。在这里没人会对枪击多想。农民经常打兔子，有钱人花大价钱来这里猎鸟。在山谷，枪声并不罕见。

我开车回里士满，享受着这一刻，感到浑身都透着兴奋，并且已经在期待下次的杀人。我离我的目标更近了。

* * *

内维尔、斯科特和拉塞尔从里斯的办案室到投降桥花了15分钟。内维尔和拉塞尔坐的是一辆警用路虎车，斯科特开自己的车。黑黄相间的警戒带已经把一辆蓝色小车周围的空旷地域隔离。两辆警用路虎停在路对面一辆红色丰田四驱车的后面。一名男警官和一名女警官正跟丰田车里的人交谈。另一名警官在安放一些大灯，这样大家都能看见办案过程。还有一位警官就站在警戒带的旁边。

第77页

“法医在来的路上。”内维尔走向他的时候他说道。

内维尔朝丰田车点点头。

“那儿发生了什么？”他问道。

“是那个女孩儿的母亲，”警官回答，“她的女儿跟男朋友出来玩儿，并说她会在 8 点之前回家吃晚饭。但她 10 点半还没有回家，她母亲出来找她。她说她知道他们经常去的地方。我们一直努力让她平静下来，但是可以理解她真的很伤心。”

“她丈夫呢？”内维尔问。

“有几个人叫他来了，也会通知男孩儿的父母。”警官回答。

第78页

“扑克牌呢？”内维尔问。

“在后座，”警官回答，“我没有碰任何东西。我一看到尸体和牌就把这里封锁了。”

“做得好，谢谢你。”内维尔转向斯科特，“我们去看看。”

他们从路虎车后备箱拿出一些白色的塑料鞋套，把它们套在自己的鞋子上。然后他们猫腰穿过警戒带，缓慢而小心地走向蓝色小车。

“你怎么想的？”内维尔问。他们绕着车走，从车窗往里面看。

“我敢说他们是从非常近的距离被射中的，”斯科特说，“但是我想我们应该等等看凯会说什么。”

正在这时一辆绿色的路虎到了，凯·哈丁从车上下来。她立刻套好鞋套加入了斯科特和内维尔。她把手伸进车窗触摸这对年轻人的脖子找寻生命迹象。

“没有奇迹发生，”她说，“但是我要例行检查。”

然后她弯腰查看他们头部的弹孔。

“他们都是从不到 1 米远的距离被射中的，”她说，“让我继续检查完，等结束的时候再多告诉你们一些。我明白这有多重要。”

第79页

“谢谢，凯。”内维尔说。

内维尔和斯科特走到警戒带外面，拉塞尔在那儿跟他们会合。

“查尔斯？”她开口道。

内维尔看着她以示回应。

“如果他又是从里士满来的……”她话没有说完。

“聪明，”内维尔看着他的手表说，“我们假设他花了一些时间想找到他在找的东西。所以首先看看是否有任何车辆被偷的报告，然后查看从大概6点钟到11点钟的监控录像。你知道要找什么。”

* * *

拉塞尔忙了一夜。首先，还没有接到任何车辆失踪的报告。下一个问题是北约克郡的监控摄像机不是警方来管理的，而是由一个本地的政府官员管理。半夜接到菲奥娜·拉塞尔的来电要那天晚上和两周前的监控录像，他不太开心。

“不能等到明天早上吗？”他困倦地抱怨道。

“当然可以，”拉塞尔回答，“我会那样跟我的上司提议。到那时我保证他会很开心地看到你到警察局来，协助我们进行调查，而且是整个晚上。”

第80页

“天哪！”拉塞尔想着不禁笑了，“我跟警察相处的时间太长了，听起来我都开始像名警察了。”

拉塞尔在一个小时内收到了通过电子邮件发过来的录像，开始工作。她先播放了一遍前一天晚上的录像，记下了每辆从里士满开往里斯和斯维尔代尔的小轿车或货车的车牌号码。然后她又看了一遍，记录下返回里士满的车。之后她将两份清单进行对比。有10辆车同时在两份清单上。她打了个哈欠，用手指拢了拢头发，然后看了看办案室另一边。内维尔和斯科特是在凌晨两点返回的。他们正在讯问室里查看一摞文件。

拉塞尔从窗边的机器里面给自己倒了一杯咖啡，又回到她的电脑前。在她弄清这10辆车车主的姓名和地址之前跟内维尔说什么都没有意义。总之，她确定杀手使用了一辆偷来的车。

在车主和车辆数据库查找了半个小时，拉塞尔得到了她想要的信息。她走到讯问室加入内维尔和斯科特。她走进去时他们抬起头。

第81页

"10个名字和地址，"她说着把一张纸放在桌上，"昨天傍晚离开里士满去往里斯方向并稍后又返回的车主。他们都有嫌疑。但是我推测车是被偷的，即使还没有关于丢车的报告。不管怎样，现在我会从前两起谋杀时的录像开始查看。"

就在这时电话响了。内维尔接起电话。

"刑侦督察内维尔，"他听了一会儿后说，"等等，凯。海伦和菲奥娜都在这儿。我打开免提。"

他按下一个按键，凯·哈丁的声音响亮而清晰地回响在房间里。

"你欠我一个人情，查尔斯，"她说，"我整夜工作为你解决这个。"

"记下了，"内维尔回答，"你发现了什么？"

"我能把死亡时间范围缩小到8点到9点30分之间，如果这个有用的话。"她回答。

"可能有用。"内维尔回答。

"他们都很年轻、健康。两个人，你知道的，死于头部中弹。"哈丁继续说。

第82页

“不错，”内维尔说，“那么子弹呢？”

“是的，子弹，”哈丁说，“出自同一把枪，都是9毫米口径，都是伊拉克造。”

“什么？”内维尔几乎吼着问的，“你是什么意思？”

“你的人在犯罪现场找到了其中一颗子弹的弹壳，”哈丁解释道，“上面有一些字。我复制后用邮件发给了我在纽卡斯尔大学的一位朋友。他是研究中东的讲师，他告诉我这些字是阿拉伯文，读作‘卡迪西亚’。我在网上查了。”

“然后呢？”内维尔问。

“卡迪西亚是伊拉克南部的一个省，”哈丁说，“但是它也是一家生产9毫米口径枪械的工厂名。这种枪叫作塔里克——基本上就是一把贝瑞塔M1951，不过是在伊拉克造的。他们从1990年之前就在制造，今天伊拉克警察还在使用。”

“伊拉克警察！”内维尔的声音中透出难以置信。

拉塞尔把一只手放在他的手臂上。

“不，”她说，“还有，全都跟军队有关。外派到伊拉克或阿富汗或者任何地方的士兵，他们都有很多机会获得枪、子弹、匕首，各种各样的东西——特别是从他们的敌人那里。”

第83页

“非常感谢，凯。”内维尔说完挂断电话，陷入沉思。他转向拉塞尔。

“所以你是说，”他说道，“一个士兵很容易持有一把塔里克9毫米口径手枪并带回英国，作为一种参战奖励。”

“没错，”拉塞尔说，“几年前我在伦敦办过一个案子，当时一个退伍军人把枪卖给了犯罪分子——他从世界各地带回的枪。”

一时间没人说话。

“我们重新调查士兵和军队。”内维尔说。他看着斯科特。“格林的名单你有何进展？”他问。

“之前我给卡特瑞克打了电话，”她说，“在格林的名单上有 6 个名字。在这些人当中，在前两起谋杀发生期间有三个人在守备部队，还有三个人最近去了阿富汗，谋杀开始之前他们就离开了。不过我想办法跟前三个士兵中的一个谈了话。他给了我另外九个跟格林交谈过的人的名字，这些人没有告诉格林他们的名字。”

第84页

斯科特看着内维尔和拉塞尔。

“但是别高兴得太早，”她警告他们，“我有种感觉，格林跟更多的人交谈过。”

“别担心，”内维尔说，“这只是一个开始。正如菲奥娜刚开始说的，我们只需要幸运一次。”

“我猜你没有弄清楚这九个人中哪些住在里士满，对吧？”拉塞尔问，“那里是车被偷的地方。”

斯科特开始翻阅她面前桌子上的文件，并把她正在找的那份抽了出来。

“不，”她回答，“我找到了。”她看着名单。“有两个人。”

她把纸转成其他人都能看到的方向。

“我会查寻车主和车辆数据库来确定他们是否有车，”拉塞尔说，“如果我们从前两起谋杀的时间开始看监控录像，那么我们有可能找得到可匹配的人。”

“去做吧。”内维尔说完，看着斯科特，“海伦，帮一下菲奥娜。

我有种感觉我们正在接近目标。”

* * *

10分钟之后，拉塞尔给了斯科特一张纸，上面写有字母和数字。

第85页

“两个车牌号码，”她说，“分别是住在里士满的两个士兵的车牌号码。我把从第二起谋杀那天开始的监控录像用邮件发送到你的电脑里了。你看那个，我会查看第一起的。”

“关于昨天晚上有车被偷的事你是对的，”斯科特坐下时说，“据报告是昨天晚上10点20分在里士满被偷的。报告可以在电脑上看到了。”

拉塞尔想了一会儿。

“车已经被找到了吗？”她问。

“我想还没有。”斯科特回答。

“让他们去盖洛菲尔德商业园碰碰运气。”拉塞尔说。

当斯科特疑惑地看着拉塞尔的时候，她说：“只是一个猜测。”

然后她用手捋了捋头发，深呼吸了一下。她看着斯科特面前纸上的两个名字和地址。

“我不太熟悉里士满，”她说，“这两个地址有在商业园附近的吗？”

“两个都不太远。”斯科特回答。

拉塞尔坐在她的电脑前。她的胳膊肘支在桌面上，双手托着下巴。她想了一阵。

第86页

“我觉得，”她开始慢慢说道，“我觉得第三起谋杀——他第一次偷车的那次——我觉得也许不像其他几次计划得那么周密。我认为他有点儿感到意外。”

斯科特看着拉塞尔。

“我还认为，”拉塞尔继续说，“他觉得自己必须立刻搬走尸体。而且第一辆车被偷的地点是商业园，因为那儿离他住的地方近。车用完后停在那儿只是试图迷惑我们。”

“对我来说这个推测听起来很有道理。”斯科特回应道。

“好，”拉塞尔说着又看了看她前面的车牌号码，“让我们瞧瞧是否能在这两个当中找到一个。”

拉塞尔和斯科特开始在她们的电脑上观看不同的录像。

45 分钟之后，拉塞尔第三次看了同一段 30 秒的录像。然后她倚靠在椅子上。

“找到你了。”她小声说。

第 7 章　里德一家

第87页

在枪击之后我想要把车停回火车站停车场。但是当我靠近的时候，我看到了一辆警车，一男一女正在跟两个警官交谈。在他们看到我之前我快速开过去，然后我开到盖洛菲尔德商业园。如果我把所有偷到的车都停在同一个地方，警察就不知道该怎么想了。

我边往家走边思考着枪击的事。在我看来这事干得漂亮：一把外国手枪，一辆偷来的车，干净利落的双杀。双杀更接近我的目标了。

我就像一台运转良好的机器，一台运转良好的杀人机器。训练——哈！我不需要为此做什么训练。这都是因为有计划，有组织，要足够勇敢去相信我能做到。要勇敢——是的。他们从不相信我够勇敢。

在回家之前，我转到一条小巷，决定一直走下去。我不想到家后还要跟谁聊天，而且我得把枪放回藏匿的地点。我会在外边再待半个小时，直到家里人全都已经上床睡觉了。

第88页

步行的时候我可以计划我的下一次冒险。它应该很快，也许就是明天。我越快达到我的目标，我的目标数，我就能越快向世界证明我的实力，他们就会越快需要我。

那么就明天，明天早上。我想进行一次溺亡行动。在斯维尔代尔和阿肯格斯代尔的河边有许多小路。出其不意地袭击某个人，把他们按到水下，感觉生命从他们身体里流逝，这应该很容易。当然，他们会回击，但是我会有所准备。我可以先击倒他们，然后把他们按在水下。或者我可以选择个头儿比我小、力气没我大的人。我仔细考虑了两种行动方案。我都喜欢。我明天做决定。

那么我计划在哪里实施呢？我在脑海中设想着沿斯维尔河从里斯到上谷地这一段。我最喜欢的地方有一条叫作巴里贝克的小溪汇入这条河。小时候我经常在那里野餐，长大后我经常在那条小路散步，我非常熟悉那个地方。

11 点过 10 分，我偷偷溜进前门。我进门后停下来听了听，安静无声。我轻轻锁上门然后进到厨房。从那儿有一扇门通往车库。

第89页

车库里装满了各种我们不想放在房子里的东西：旧箱子、干衣机、两辆自行车、一台坏了的电视、手提箱，各种废品。手提箱被放在屋顶下的一个平台上。我爬上去打开了其中一个。里面是一个金属盒子，金属盒里是一块布料。我从口袋里掏出枪，用布料裹住枪，把枪放进盒子，再把盒子放回手提箱。这是他放枪的地方——但是他不知道我知道了！

今晚我会为明天的冒险在我的地图上贴一枚标签。你可能会认为我过于自信，但是我不这样认为，我知道我不会失败。

* * *

“艾伦·里德陆军少校，”菲奥娜·拉塞尔边在一张纸上写边说，“拥有一辆红色福特福克斯，KV06EUU。我看到这辆车在第一起谋杀案发生时的凌晨 5 点 25 分从里士满朝斯维尔代尔方向开出，并在 11 点 40 分返回里士满。”

海伦·斯科特低头看着她的车牌号码清单。

“我看到同一辆车在第二起谋杀当天下午 4 点 30 分出现了。”她说。

第90页

“我们已经对上号了，查尔斯。”拉塞尔喊内维尔。

内维尔来到拉塞尔的桌前。

“地址呢？”他问道。

拉塞尔把她刚才一直在记东西的纸递给他。

“里士满夸里路。那里离盖洛菲尔德商业园近吗？”她问道。

“非常近。”内维尔说。他看着斯科特。“快点儿，我们走。”他说。他转向拉塞尔。“你也来。我想知道你的想法。”

半个小时之后，早上 7 点 30 分，斯科特把警车停在了夸里路上一栋看起来别致的石屋外。前面花园被悉心照料得干净整齐。房前私人车道上没有那辆红色的福特福克斯，街上也没有。内维尔、斯科特和拉塞尔走到前门。内维尔按了门铃。

有人来开门的声音，然后门开了。是一位60多岁的白发老妇人开的门，她睡衣外面披着家居服。

“什么事？”她问道。

内维尔举起他的警官证。

第91页

“刑侦督察内维尔，北约克郡警察局，”他说，“这位是刑侦警长斯科特，这位是拉塞尔女士，警方案情分析专家。我们要找一位叫艾伦·里德的陆军少校。”

女人看起来很担心。

“艾伦？”她问，“你们找他有什么事？”

“这恐怕不能跟您说，”内维尔说，“也许我们可以进去。”

女人把门开大了一些。

“哦，是的，”她说，“我想这样更好。到客厅里来，我去叫艾伦。”

女人把内维尔、斯科特和拉塞尔领进房子前部一个明亮的房间。他们站着环顾四周：舒适的家具、谷地的图片、家庭照片、角落里一台落地式大摆钟。

“艾伦！”他们听到女人朝楼上喊，“这儿有几位警官要见你。你可以自己下来吗？”

“没问题，妈妈。”他答道。

有人慢慢下楼的声音传来。然后门开了。女人回到客厅，身后跟了一个30岁出头走得很慢的男人，胳膊下各拄着一只拐杖，支撑着他行走。他的右腿是正常的，左腿没了，裤腿在膝盖以上被裁掉了。

第92页

他环顾房间。

“不好意思我得坐下。”他说。他移动到一个颜色鲜艳的扶手椅边，一屁股坐下，把拐杖放在旁边的地上。

“路边的炸弹炸的，是在阿富汗受的伤。”他解释道，“我还算幸运，我们有两个人死了。我正在等着装上一条新腿。”

内维尔、斯科特和拉塞尔面面相觑。这个人明显不会是那个杀手。

“我能为你们做些什么？”里德看着内维尔问。

“你是艾伦·里德陆军少校。”内维尔说。

“是的。”

“你有一辆红色的福特福克斯。”内维尔说。

“是的。”

“车在哪里？”内维尔问。

“不是停在房子前面吗？”里德问。

“不，不在。”内维尔说。

“哦，特里很可能开出去了。”里德回答。

“特里？”内维尔问。

“我弟弟。”里德解释说。

拉塞尔注意到她旁边的小桌子上的一张照片。两个年轻人和一个老妇人：艾伦和特里·里德，还有他们的母亲。她拿起这张照片递给了内维尔。

第93页

“你弟弟也参军了吗？”内维尔看着照片问。

“不，他是一个园丁，兼职的。他给住在里士满不同地方的几个人干活儿。”里德回答。

“你去过阿富汗也去过伊拉克吗？”内维尔问。

“是的，”里德回答，“两次。”

“你有枪吗？”斯科特问。

“没有，”里德说，“显然我知道怎么开枪。我服役的时候有一把，但是我们回国的时候不准许把枪带出卡特瑞克驻地。”

有段短暂的沉默。

“那么，一把塔里克9毫米口径的枪呢？”斯科特问。

“你什么意思？”里德问。

“我的意思是，一样你带回家能使你回忆起在伊拉克的日子的东西，一件战利品。”斯科特说。

“里德陆军少校，”没等里德回答，内维尔说，“我们正在调查在谷地发生的系列谋杀案。你应该已经在报纸上读到了，也看到了新闻报道。我期待你的诚实回答。”

里德深吸一口气。

第94页

“是的，”他说，“我确实有一把塔里克9毫米口径的枪。但是，我确定，其他几百名军人和退伍军人也都有。我的那把藏得很好，从我把它带回家以后就从来没有用过。”

“枪在哪里？”内维尔问，“我们想看看。”

里德拾起拐杖艰难地站了起来。

“我带你们去看。”他说。

内维尔朝斯科特点头，她跟着里德走出房间。

交谈中拉塞尔一直在环顾房间。她看到了更多的家庭照片，开始对它们更感兴趣起来：一个婴儿、一个小男孩儿和他们的父母；两个少年；两个年轻人和他们的母亲；穿着军装的比现在年轻的艾伦·里德。事实上有三四张里德的军装照，但是没有他弟弟最近的照片。

拉塞尔看着里德的母亲，她一直坐在沙发上，但没有参与谈话。

“里德夫人，”她开口道，“特里比艾伦小吗？”

“是的，”里德夫人回答，“他们俩差 4 岁。”

“特里也想参军吗？”拉塞尔问。

第95页

“哦，是的，”里德夫人回答，“在艾伦当兵期间，特里开口就是这个——他们一起当兵该多好。他总是想做艾伦做的事。你知道，就像弟弟经常做的那样，他仰慕哥哥。”

“那么发生了什么呢？”拉塞尔问。

“唉，他开始训练了，”里德夫人看着地板说，“后来军方决定不要他了。”

拉塞尔什么也没说。她只是疑惑地看着里德夫人。

最后这位满头白发的女人抬头看着拉塞尔。

“他们说这跟他的心理有关，心理方面的问题，”她说，“我不是太明白。他很健康、强壮。他通过了所有的体能测试，通过了所有的考试。之后他们说他‘不适合现代军队的生活’。”

“他怎么想的？”拉塞尔问。

“唉，你能想象得到，”里德夫人说，“参军曾经是他的人生志向，是他的梦想，突然一夜间就破灭了。这对他来说很可怕，他感到非常非常失望——事实上不只是失望，还有愤怒。”

第96页

拉塞尔看着内维尔，然后视线回到里德夫人。

“你认为这件事完全改变了他吗？”她问，“没能参军。”

里德夫人想了一会儿。

“是的，”她说，“我认为这件事确实改变了他。他以前更开朗，对人更友好。他现在更加封闭，有点儿活在自己的世界里。”

正在这时客厅的门开了，斯科特回到房间里，里德在她后面。斯科特的手里有一把枪。

“一把塔里克 9 毫米口径，”她说，“最近被使用过。”

里德夫人发出声音，她的手捂住嘴。

“你们不会认为……”她开口说，但她没有讲完。

里德的脸色惨白。他看起来在发抖。

“不可能是特里，”他说，“他不知道我有枪。我从来没有告诉过他。他不是……”他也说不出话来了。

“我们要查看他的房间。”内维尔说。

“当然，”里德夫人声音颤抖着说，“在楼上的右边。”

内维尔给斯科特一个暗示，示意她跟里德一家待在一起，然后他和拉塞尔上了楼。

第97页

“我们要尽快找到他，”拉塞尔跟在内维尔身后爬楼梯的时候说，“我觉得他又出去杀人了。”

“今天？”内维尔说。

“是的，”拉塞尔回答，“今天。按照惯例，一旦连环杀手开始作案，谋杀案发生的时间间隔会越来越短。就像是毒品，他们会越来越需要它。”

特里·里德的房间异常整齐：床铺特别整洁，桌椅整齐排列，钢笔和铅笔排成一线，书柜里的书按大小排列，还有一个放衣服的柜子。

内维尔打开了衣柜的门。拉塞尔从书桌的抽屉开始查找。两分钟之后她打开了一幅地图，是在下面第三个抽屉找到的。

“这里。”她说。内维尔凑过来看。

“看看蓝色贴签所在的位置，”拉塞尔指着地图说，“第一起谋杀、第二起、第三起、第四起和第五起。”每一个贴签都贴在一起谋杀案发生的地方。

“这儿还有一个，”内维尔指着另一个说，“巴尼贝克。他一定去了那里。”

第 8 章　缉拿凶手

第99页

我今天一早就离开了家。天上有乌云，但是看起来好像等会儿就会放晴。今天我开了艾伦的车。我不想太频繁地偷车。科技在当今很发达，你永远无法知道警方可能会发现什么。我把车开到里斯，然后停在村庄中间。然后我朝被称为巴尼贝克的小溪出发。小路穿过旷野通往斯维尔河，然后沿着河岸，穿过一些树木。

就在巴尼贝克的前方，小路越来越接近河流。小路右边有一堵干砌石墙，河就在左边几米远的地方，河岸两边长着挺拔的树木。现在我到了巴尼贝克汇入河流的地方等待。

这是一个隐蔽的地方。这就是我选择这里的原因。还有一个原因就是这里有跨过小溪的踏脚石。

在我和艾伦小的时候妈妈经常带我们来这儿。我们会从里斯走过来，在这里停下野餐，打水漂。之后我们或者沿原路返回，或者，当我们大一点儿的时候，我们会继续走到斯卡巴沃斯桥，从河的对岸返回里斯。那是一段快乐的时光。

第100页

我18个月大的时候父亲就去世了，所以我完全不了解他。艾伦也几乎不记得他了。妈妈独自把我们养大。即使她一视同仁，我还是感觉她最爱的是我。艾伦总是和他的朋友出去踢足球，骑车，攀岩或……做一些事情。我大部分时间都跟妈妈在一起，我们总是很亲近。

我观察河边来回的路，还没有人过来。我在墙后找了一个可以藏身的地方。如果有一对或者一群行人走过，我就藏起来。我在等独自来的人。

尽管我是妈妈的最爱，但我总是嫉妒艾伦。他是我们之中的成功者。他参军的时候妈妈感到很骄傲。我知道我也必须要试试。

我又看了看两边的路。我能看到远处有一行四人从里斯沿着小路走过来。我快速躲进藏身之处。这群人花了15分钟到达这里，然后走过去。我又等了5分钟，等他们走远。然后我又出来朝两个方向查看，没有人来。

第101页

我开始军队训练时一切进展顺利。体能训练上我一点儿问题也没有，通过了考试。事实上，我是高分通过的。但是之后的心理测试：那些问题好像并没有正确或错误答案，是关于现役、上前线的问题。然后他们告诉我说我不合适。起初，我简直不敢相信。我唯一想做的就是成为一名军人。军队拒绝了我——每天早上我怎么能够正视镜子中的自己？我做了我唯一能做的事情。我决定向他们证明，他们错了。

我又观察河边两个方向的路。大概 100 米开外有个红色的东西。我通过望远镜看到一个穿着红色厚夹克的女人。她从斯卡巴沃斯沿着小路过来。她独自一人。

我伸开双手又握住。

就是她。

我准备好了。

* * *

斯科特开车，内维尔和拉塞尔坐在车后座。内维尔拿出手机打了个电话。拉塞尔听了一会儿他下达指示，然后向前探身，从前座拿起一张地图。她知道巴尼贝克在哪里——在里斯和哈拉夫之间的斯维尔河沿岸——她自己走过很多次。但是她不确定最快到达的路是哪一条。她展开地图。

第102页

从内维尔打电话时所说的话判断，拉塞尔很清楚内维尔对这个地区相当熟悉。她没有再听而是看着地图。从里斯到他们认为特里·里德所在的地方的小路很长。如果把车停在哈拉夫外的公路上然后步行走过两片田野会更快一些。她刚要跟内维尔指出这一点的时候，就听到他说："我要三个人，全副武装，在里斯等候，坐小车，不要用路虎车。我们经过的时候接上他们。我们到巴尼贝克最近的路是哈拉夫外的那条。然后我们从那儿步行。"他挂掉电话。

拉塞尔看着内维尔。他一脸疲惫，甚至筋疲力尽，但是他眼中闪着兴奋的光芒，因为他们离要找的人近了。这个案子跟她曾经处理过的其他的连环杀手调查案一样。谋杀的时间间隔越来越短；警察工作的时间越来越长，查看的信息越来越多；然后在最后关头，一切都似乎陷入了疯狂。

第103页

斯科特打开蓝色警灯，从里士满到里斯只用了17分钟。一辆没有标记的警车正在巴克旅店的对面等着。她在那辆车旁边停下，内维尔打开窗户。

“跟着我们。”他跟司机说。

5分钟之后，他们停在尽可能远离路边的地方，就在哈拉夫村外。拉塞尔明白了内维尔要一辆小车而不是路虎的原因。路虎是高大的交通工具，从河边的干砌石墙上可以看到车顶。真是聪明。

警察和拉塞尔都下了车。手枪被交到内维尔和斯科特的手上。内维尔看着拉塞尔。

“你留在这儿。”他说，“你不是警察，我不想要你接触这些。”

“没问题。”她说。她希望她能帮助内维尔和斯科特及时到达正确的地点拯救某人的生命。但是她很开心不用比这更接近一位连环杀手了。

* * *

斯科特打开大门，5名警官进入田野。她关上大门。田野远处有几只绵羊，即使有个杀手逍遥法外，农民看到羊跑了也不会高兴的。

第104页

很快，警察穿过了田野，弯腰前进以便不被看见。田野尽头是另一扇门。他们轻轻地把它打开又关上，然后跑过另一片田野，到了墙脚。当他们到达墙根的时候都压低着身子。斯科特环顾四周，表情坚定，嘴唇紧闭，持枪准备射击。

内维尔朝斯科特点头。她从墙头看过去。她用5秒钟弄清了情况。有踏脚石横过巴尼贝克。一名男子正站在小溪的一侧。他背对着她，但是她肯定那人就是特里·里德。小溪的另一侧是一名步行者，一个穿着红色厚夹克的女人。她离踏脚石有几米远，正向他们走来。里德伸出一只手帮她踏过石头。她抓住了伸过来的手。她这么做的时候，抬头看到了斯科特。

里德意识到有人在他的身后。他突然转身直勾勾地盯着斯科特。

第105页

没有时间去想接下来要做什么了。斯科特从墙头举起枪对准了里德。

“警察！”她大喊，“放开那个女人的手，别动。”

里德行动迅速。他快速穿过小溪朝女人奔过去，将他抓着的女人的一只手扭到她的身后，他的另一只胳膊卡住她的脖子。

“站在那儿，”他朝斯科特喊，“不要再靠近了。”

斯科特知道内维尔可以听到他们的对话。他小声说话并用手指示，他会让其他警察从后面接近里德——很有可能一个穿过河流往更接近里斯的方向；其他两个回到公路上，绕到里德的身后。她知道他会藏在墙后。

“别做蠢事，”斯科特说，“放开她，我们可以谈谈。”

“哈！”里德大笑，然后开始朝后移动。他身后有一堵墙和一个通往田野的开口。斯科特看得出他想要做什么，但是她没有办法阻止他。

第106页

突然，里德从墙头捡起一块石头击打女人的头部。随着女人倒下，他转身快速跑到田野里去了。

第107页

“快，”斯科特边朝内维尔和其他人大喊，边跑过踏脚石来到受伤的女人旁边，“他跑了，朝公路方向。”内维尔转身跑了起来。

* * *

起初菲奥娜坐在车里，但是在秋日阳光的照耀下，车里温度很快升高了。她下车站在内维尔、斯科特和其他警察首先穿过的门旁边。她的胳膊肘搭在门顶，看着下面的河。几分钟之前有几声喊叫声，但没有枪击声。她不知道他们是否已经找到了里德。几分钟之后，她看到两名警察从里斯方向爬过了那堵干砌石墙下到田野的右边。看起来就好像他们确实找到了人。

她刚要回车里去，这时她感觉到有什么硬东西戳着她的背。

“小心一点儿。”一个声音说道，“这可是一把枪，我可不想用到它。”

拉塞尔感觉全身在冒汗。

“你想干什么？”她问。她知道他就是里德。

“钥匙在车上吗？”里德问。

第108页

“我想在吧。”

“打开乘客那侧的车门，慢慢坐进去。”他说。

拉塞尔侧身去拉车门。她看不到枪，但是她能感觉到它紧紧顶着她的侧肋。

从眼角余光她可以看到他，这个她一直在找的人。他很高，看起来很累。他有一双小眼睛、短下巴、黑色直发。

“放松点儿，”她说，“我不是警察，但是我可以帮你。”

“别说话，”他回答，“慢慢坐进车里。”

慢慢地，拉塞尔坐到乘客座上。里德的枪仍紧紧顶着她的侧肋。

“现在移到驾驶座上去。”里德命令道。

拉塞尔正准备移动时，听到一阵吵声。她看向左边，内维尔和斯科特出现在进入田野的门边，手里握着枪。

“放开她，”内维尔说，他的枪指着里德，“慢慢往后退，否则我们开枪了。”

“我也会开枪的，”里德说，“你们肯定也不想让这个女人死掉。”

第109页

拉塞尔看到内维尔和斯科特交换眼神。

“你从哪里找到的枪，里德？”斯科特问。她盯着里德，然后转向拉塞尔，两人视线相会。

“菲奥娜，他真的有枪吗？”她问。

拉塞尔迅速思考。她感觉到了枪，但是她并没有看到枪。这不是塔里克 9 毫米口径枪——今天早上早些时候他们还在他家看到过。他还有一把枪吗？她应该冒险吗？她侧过身，用双手用力推里德的胸口。他从车旁摔出去，背部着地。他手里是一根木头冒充的枪。

内维尔和斯科特瞬间穿过门。内维尔用枪顶住里德的脑袋；斯科特粗暴地把他的两臂扭到他背后，然后戴上手铐。

里德开始戴着手铐挣扎。

“放我走！”他大叫，脑袋不停地晃着，“我需要完成这次行动，我需要达到我的目标，我需要向他们证明我能做什么。”

内维尔、斯科特和里德看看彼此。

“军队，”里德继续说，仍然想挣脱双手，“我需要向他们证明我已经具备他们的要求。我需要向他们证明我可以杀人，而且我很擅长。我需要向他们证明我就是他们想要的那种人。”

第110页

内维尔只是摇摇头。

* * *

那天下午晚些时候，内维尔、斯科特和拉塞尔在半月酒店的酒吧里。里斯纪念堂已经被清空了，警察带过来的所有桌椅、电脑和电话都搬走了。特里·里德已经被审问过，被带到了里士满警察局后还会被再审。海伦·斯科特已经去里士满再次跟里德的母亲和哥哥交谈，然后她回到里斯。内维尔已经跟记者交谈过，并且接受了电视和广播的采访。

内维尔从吧台端来三个杯子，然后放在他们坐的桌子上：啤酒是给他自己的，白葡萄酒是给斯科特的，红葡萄酒是给拉塞尔的。

“感谢上帝，都结束了。”他重重坐下来说。

“是啊。”斯科特赞同道。

“就是因为军队没要他。”内维尔说。

第111页

“嗯，在他眼里军队不要他是因为他们认为他不会杀人。”拉塞尔解释说，“他杀人是为了证明他会杀人。每次他都用一种不同的方式杀人以此证明他有多擅长。”

“疯了，”内维尔说，“完全疯了。”

“是的，”拉塞尔表示赞同，“但是对他来说这是符合逻辑的。他只是想向军队证明他们犯了一个错误。连环杀手一般都认为他们做事很有逻辑。”

“然而是一种疯狂的逻辑。”斯科特说。

“是的。”拉塞尔回答。

“这是什么？你的第三个还是第四个连环杀手？”内维尔问。

“第三个。”拉塞尔回答。她喝了一点儿葡萄酒。“在某些方面三个人完全不同，但其他方面很相似。”

“为什么这样说呢?”

“嗯，第一个，”拉塞尔开始说道，“是一个女人，事实上是一个护士，她杀死的是一些她去上门护理的家里的老人。在她看来他们都老到不能自理，所以不应该活着。”

拉塞尔又喝了一些酒。

第112页

“第二个，”她继续说，“是一个男人，他的女朋友大概5年前离开了他。从那以后，他跟女性相处就有了很大障碍。问题越积越多，最后他开始杀害20多岁金色头发的年轻女性。那些女孩儿让他想起他的前女友。”

“而现在一个家伙想要向军队证明他知道怎样杀人，这样的话他们就会让他参军。”斯科特补充道。

“千真万确。”拉塞尔回答。

“那么他们相似的地方在哪儿呢?”内维尔问。

“他们都表明了一件小事就能打破人的心理平衡，产生倒错，”拉塞尔回答，“入伍没有成功，跟女朋友分手，从事一份你本应该去帮助别人最后却变成了仇恨别人的工作——这些都是人们在生命中的某段时间经常会经历的事情——”

“但是这些通常并不会使他们变成杀手。”斯科特插嘴道。

“是的，不会，”拉塞尔说，“正常人可以应付过去。他们继续生活。他们换一份工作，他们去交一个新的女朋友。但是对于极少数人来说，这足以打破他们的心理平衡。他们产生了一种奇怪的、恶毒的、谋杀的逻辑，驱使他们去杀人。而且，一旦杀了一次……”

第113页

拉塞尔停下来，低头看着她的杯子。

斯科特把手放在拉塞尔的胳膊上。

“现在都结束了，菲奥娜。”她说。

拉塞尔抬起头。

“是的，结束了，”她附和说，“直到下一次。”